Improving Mental Health Outcomes Through Case Management Services

The Cog of the Wheel

by

Dr. Lorena Fulton, LCSW

Contents

Chapter 1: THE EVOLUTION OF PROFESSIONAL HELPING AND CASE MANAGEMENT 1

    Roots of Advocacy 1

Chapter 2: MICRO AND MACRO SYSTEMS OF CARE 6

    Introduction 6

    The Micro Tier of the Ecological Social System 9

    The Macro Tier of the Ecological Social System 12

    Connecting Advocacy and Collaboration for Professional Helpers 13

    Chapter Summary 14

Chapter 3: ADVOCACY IN CASE MANAGEMENT SERVICES 16

    Introduction 16

    Professional Case Management 17

    Joining with Vulnerable People in Need 19

    Discussion 21

    Elements of Advocacy in Case Management 21

    Question 21

    Conclusion 23

Chapter 4: ADVOCACY FOCUSED 24

    Introduction 24

    Discussion 24

    What is Professional Collaboration? 25

    The Purpose of Professional Collaboration 26

    Initiation Collaboration of an Advocacy-Focused Collaboration 28

    Goals of the Collaboration 29

    Political Influences 30

Chapter Summary 31

Chapter 5: INDIVIDUAL CASE (MICRO SYSTEM):
COLLABORATION IN CASE MANAGEMENT 33

Introduction 33

Case Collaboration 33

Presenting Problems 35

Case Scenario 36

Interventions and Supports 37

Strengths-Based Approach and Building Resilience 38

Conclusion 40

Chapter 6: INDIRECT (MACRO SYSTEM) INTERVENTIONS IN
CASE MANAGEMENT 41

The Evolution of Social Policy 41

Advocacy Drives Reform and Programming 44

Case Example 46

Conclusion 49

Chapter 7: COMBINING MICRO AND MACRO SYSTEM
ADVOCACY AND COLLABORATION 51

Introduction 51

Building a Healthy Community 52

The Shift from Micro to Macro Advocacy 55

Community Building Efforts 56

Bringing Micro Advocacy to the Macro Tier 58

Conclusion 61

Chapter 8: APPLICATION: INTEGRATING MEDICAL CARE WITH MENTAL HEALTH TREATMENT 62

Introduction 62

Struggling Healthcare System in the US 64

Evolution of Integrated Health and Mental Health Care 65

Evidenced-Based Practice for Integrating Mental and Physical Healthcare 67

Person-Centered Approach 68

Chapter Summary 68

References 70

Chapter 1

THE EVOLUTION OF PROFESSIONAL HELPING AND CASE MANAGEMENT

This chapter summarizes the evolution of professional helping from neighbor helping neighbor to coordinated support and advocacy, the introduction of state-level welfare policy, and the introduction of federal welfare social policy. What began as a social obligation based on self-preservation through community preservation, neighbor-helping-neighbor gave birth to compassionate benevolence that singled out the occasional committed helpers. Larger community members began referring people in need to identified helpers who stockpiled resources and accepted donations. Over time, a formal system of gathering and helping grew into charitable organizations, which included almshouses, orphanages, mental hospitals, and food banks.

Roots of Advocacy

Christian principles and benevolence are paramount in religious beliefs about "help to those in need" in Westernized cultures. Christian culture had a profound influence on Western cultures from the 17th Century, based on governmental reform measures combining "reason with revelation" that were based on Christian principles. This movement promoted libraries and schools throughout Europe and the New World, and it also promoted the idea that Catholics and Protestants work in unison to help people in need (Roberson, 2016). As these societies progressed with government intervention, a formalized institution -based welfare system developed.

Other religions, such as Islam, which promotes benevolence toward other Muslims, and Buddhism, which promotes benevolence to anyone in need, concur with Westernized views about helping people in need and advocating for vulnerable populations. It is obvious that the world is not black or white and suffering is a part of it all. The metaphysics of tawhid finds its most appropriate ethical expression in suffering, for the virtues of compassion and mercy, generosity and love become the hallmarks of the character of one who has truly realized Unity (Shah-Kazemi, 2022).

As politicians agreed, formal social policy evolved into a network of provisions and services to meet basic needs. In the US during the late 1800s, people began to migrate away from rural areas and into cities. This was the result of industrialization and specialization of labor. This change in demographics resulted in a need for policies to help our old, disabled, blind, and poor because neighbor-to-neighbor assistance evaporated in a large urban environment. As the US grew, including the influx of immigrants, we depended on our government to take control and develop more and even better policies for the unfortunate. As time progressed throughout our history, we began increasingly to depend on the federal and state governments to make and reform our welfare policies to take care of our needy (Abramovitz, 2022).

As societies became more organized, we developed a complex system of social structures to improve communities, and this occurred around the globe. Today, incorporating help such as CTC (Communities To Care) for the needy into the social structure ensures that a community will remain stable by solidifying the foundation of the community and generate positive net benefits to society as a whole (Kuklinski, Oesterle, Briney, & Hawkins, 2021). Communities that fail to meet the needs of the most vulnerable put themselves at risk of festering social problems that erode the social structure. The nature and scope of the field of professional helping varies due to its grass roots foundation. In recent decades, we have seen an attempt to focus and streamline the base of knowledge in the field into a more usable and standardized form. Homeostasis includes organizational and social structures communicating to achieve equilibrium, which is crucial for maintaining stability and functionality within complex systems (Alderwick, Hutchings, Briggs, & Mays, 2021; Dhir et al., 2020).

As local communities developed structured governments, they began to collaborate with charitable organizations and allocate resources to public relief. By the late 1920s, most US states had funded assistance for mothers with dependent children and the elderly. The Great Depression overcame most of these programs because revenue was down, and basic needs skyrocketed (Fishback, 2020).

(Photo from Public Domain)

The historical evolution of U.S. social policy, particularly regarding entitlement programs, can be traced back to significant legislative milestones during the Great Depression. Initially, the Emergency Relief and Construction Act of 1932 marked the federal government's first substantial intervention in welfare. This initiative was significantly expanded the following year with the enactment of the Federal Emergency Relief Act of 1933. Although these programs were intended as temporary solutions to immediate economic hardships, they laid the philosophical and operational groundwork for modern social policies. These early acts introduced a cultural shift towards expecting and accepting federal involvement in welfare, setting precedents for the entitlement programs observed today (Fishback, 2020).

A great part of the political debate about how the government should be involved in providing for the needy includes a philosophical debate about what aid should look like. On one end of the spectrum, politicians believe that people in need require only money to meet their needs, and on the other end is the belief that well-trained administrators who are working toward better outcomes can provide people in need with the skills, access, and insight to eventually provide for themselves (Hower, 2016). Another part of the debate surrounds political views about the role of government in society. One side believes that the role of the government is to protect citizens and not be involved with provisions or morality. The other side believes that the government should regulate all aspects of society, including the provision of basic needs.

Today, the federal and state governments share the responsibility for providing basic needs with intricate human service agencies. to a great extent of this is accomplished through a contract for the private agency to administer government-funded (taxpayer-supported) benefits and services. Other private programs solicit private (non-government) funds to provide benefits and services through philanthropic means. These private agencies may be for-profit businesses or not-for-profit and run more like a charity. Either way, private agencies seek to improve public policy, influence governmental actions, and protect individual rights. They also cultivate social change by improving the lives of service users and by educating the public about needs, solutions, and services.

The various fields of professional helping include nursing, social work, medicine, counseling, and religious ministry.

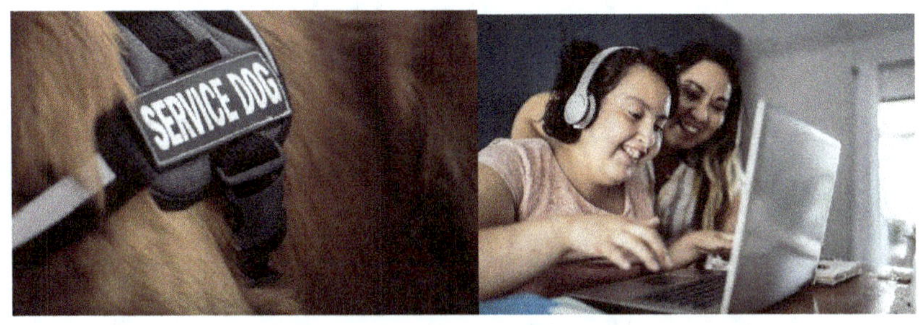

Our purpose, in general, is to enhance human well-being with a special focus on the vulnerable and oppressed (National Association of Social Workers, 2021). Through the promotion of wellbeing by building healthy communities, pairing advocacy and collaboration promotes positive change with a team effort. Professional advocacy is constrained when embarked on by a single professional or agency, and collaboration lacks authenticity when it fails to promote social justice. The role of professional helping in these interactions is to develop better adaptations for the person or group and better environments for all. Mental health service delivery is contained within in this category.

Chapter 2

MICRO AND MACRO SYSTEMS OF CARE

Introduction

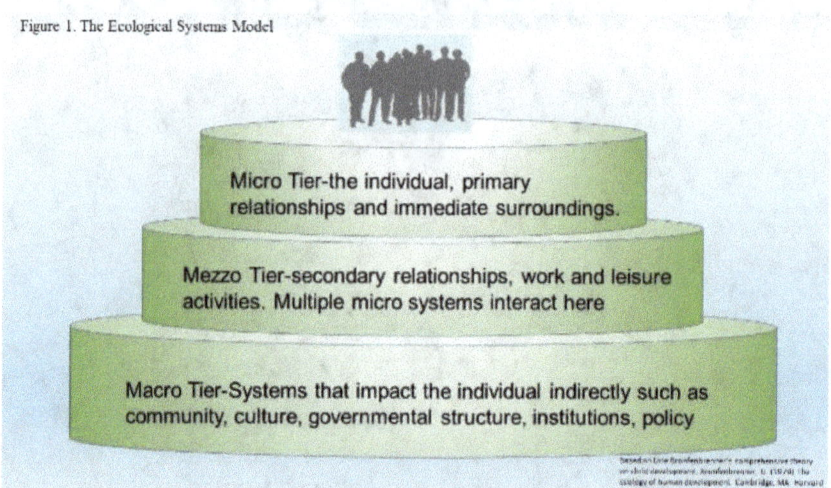

Figure 1. The Ecological Systems Model

The ecological systems model of social functioning provides a strong foundation for professional helping. Figure 1 illustrates a simple overview of the theory. The detailed Ecological Systems Theory, which is widely applied to clinical research and intervention, may include up to three middle for "mezzo" tiers. Each tier includes smaller systems that interact with each other to make up a social environment. These systems include, for example, the family, the extended family, the community, the school system, the healthcare system, and the elected government. Each system is comprised of interrelated components with fluid behavior patterns (see Figure 2.). Great study and consideration are devoted to the balance of genetic and biological influences versus environmental factors and the role that each play in the influence of overt behavior. For this, we are considering biological and environmental factors as part of the whole person who exists within a social and physical environment.

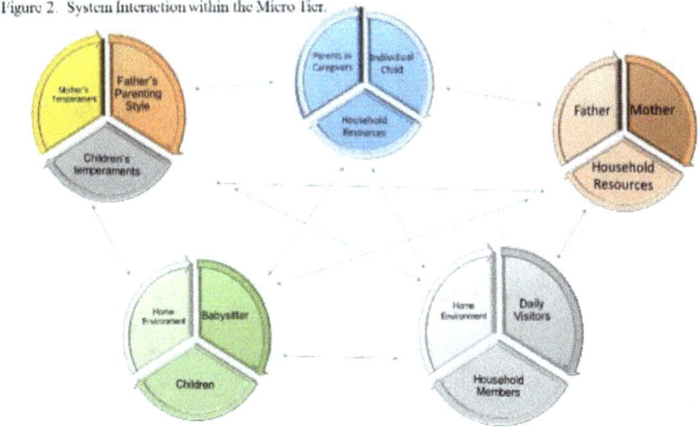

Figure 2. System Interaction within the Micro Tier.

This model considers the fluctuating relationship between the parts and the systems and then categorizes systems into tiers by their level of influence on the individual or family. All social systems reach an equilibrium, or balance, which may be adaptive in nature or may be maladaptive in nature. Resilient systems are generally adaptive with positive outcomes, and maladaptive systems are generally at risk of negative outcomes. Stressors or resilience factors in one or more micro systems influence the equilibrium or balance, which is essentially the day-to-day quality of life to which the person or family has become accustomed. Collaboration between professionals from multiple disciplines is, in effect, a conduit for advocacy in the interest of increasing resiliency.

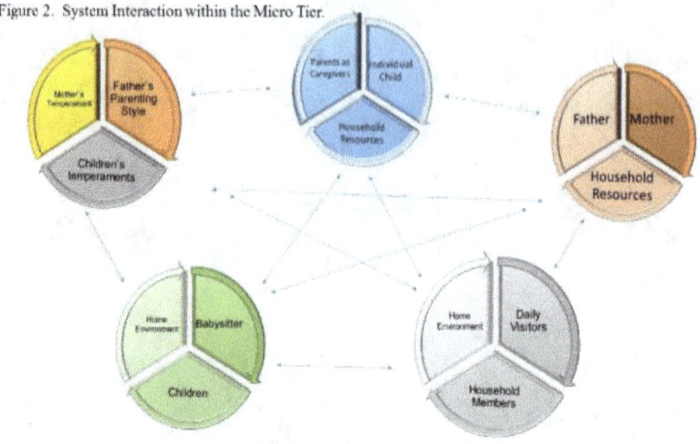
Figure 2. System Interaction within the Micro Tier.

Systems of care are simplified with the two tiers of a continuum, which include the micro and macro tier, often referred to as micro and macro practice or clinical and community practice. The micro tier of this model includes the person's strengths and weaknesses as well as people in their immediate surroundings, such as caregivers, household members, close extended family members, and close friends. The macro tier includes neighborhoods, the languages spoken, the political context, and institutional systems (schools, hospitals, religious institutions, etc.). Both tiers have an impact on a person's development. Professional interventions on the micro level work with individuals and families directly, and our work on the macro level is with policy, agencies, and funding.

In summary, this theory suggests that "every interaction, decision, and event that occurs in a person's life will have a short-term impact on them. It will either be positive, negative, or neutral. The response to those impacts create additional impacts. This process continues throughout the life of the child and affects how they will make choices and respond to environmental stimuli when they are an adult." (*Urie Bronfenbrenner's Ecological Systems Theory*, 2016)

As professional helpers promote our effectiveness and streamline the communication of the knowledge base, we find that improving outcomes in the field feeds positive social change. In other words, we can duplicate and expand on something that works when we prove that it works. The overall vision of professional helping is to enhance human well-being with a special focus on the vulnerable and oppressed (National Association of Social Workers, 2021). We work toward this goal by promoting the well-being of the entire society through building healthy communities; pairing advocacy and collaboration is an effective and efficient method of doing so.

The role of professional helping in these interactions is to develop better adaptations for the person or group and better environments for all. Collaborating with other professionals within and outside of our own field creates a network of information about system resources, limitations, and specific case scenarios.

Applying collaboration of specific services to other formal social structures such as the legal system, the educational system, health systems, and religion combines resources to create a more efficient micro-system impact. Linking our services to other formal social structures, such as the legal system, the educational system, health systems, and religion, combine resources to create a more efficient macro-system impact. Effectively linking our field to other professional fields weaves a thread of interdependence into the grid of our community's foundation that ensures the health of our thriving community, which is the goal of advocacy.

The Micro Tier of the Ecological Social System

An individual person is a complex being. Each of us has physical characteristics, skills, preferences, and fears. We exist in a social environment with close relationships, acquaintances, positive relationships, and negative ones. Our environment also contains resources, interactions within close personal relationships, and cultural influences. We live in a complex and ever-changing system.

The micro tier of the ecological, social system considers the interactions of parts and systems within the immediate environment of the individual. Often, this perspective considers immediate families or small groups in place of an individual. Professional helpers analyze strengths and limitations within the micro tier that result in adaptive or maladaptive outcomes. We want to know what, in the person's environment, helps them to adapt in a positive manner and what may result in more negative influences (maladaptive outcomes). We want to increase adaptive factors and decrease maladaptive factors. Advocating for individuals and families through the conduit of collaboration between professionals with expertise in medicine, education, law, and social functioning accomplishes this desire.

Consider a family of four living in poverty with a child who suffers from chronic and severe ear infections. Upon visiting the family, we find that the electricity is often of due to lack of payment, a debris-filled carpet because the vacuum is broken, dirty laundry piled four feet high, and an empty refrigerator. Obvious limitations for the patient with ear infections include a cold house, poor nutrition, and poor personal hygiene. Delving further, we find supportive grandparents and an uncle who lives two blocks away. In increasing adaptive strengths, we can arrange for the uncle to provide transportation to the food bank, for the children to stay with grandparents when the power is off, and for the family to borrow the uncle's vacuum once per week to clean the carpet.

Note that the child's chronic ear infections impact his attendance at school, his focus when he attends, and his ability to positively interact with his peers because he does not feel well. The illness also affects his mother's ability to go to work and puts her at risk of losing her job. The stress level of the family is increased. This results in marital discourse and a lack of nurturing the children. The family has adopted an ineffective strategy that has resulted in maladaptive homeostasis or balance by avoiding supportive extended family and failing to provide care and supervision to the children. They exist on a day-to-day basis and are accustomed to a high level of stress and unhappiness.

"The **homeostasis** of a family or system is a statement of what fit defined the family or system. It is not a statement that the fit was healthy or functional or good or positive. Homeostasis, conceptually, is neutral"

(Smith, 2017).

As professional helpers who advocate for the family, we must facilitate collaboration between the pediatrician, the school, child protection services, and extended family. In addition to environmental improvements, this collaboration may result in recommending that other adults in the family alternate staying home with the sick child, and marital counseling. The family physician might link the family to a social worker, for example, who then collaborates with the school. By addressing the microsystem as a whole and not just the symptoms of the parts, we seek long-term solutions that will improve the overall strength and resilience of the family.

As professional helpers who provide direct practice in the micro tier, we are influential in improving the quality of life of our patients, clients, and beneficiaries. **Our role is to help the person or family improve their quality of life by changing factors within the system from maladaptive factors to adaptive or helpful factors.** We do this with the support of systems withing the macro tier.

The Macro Tier of the Ecological Social System

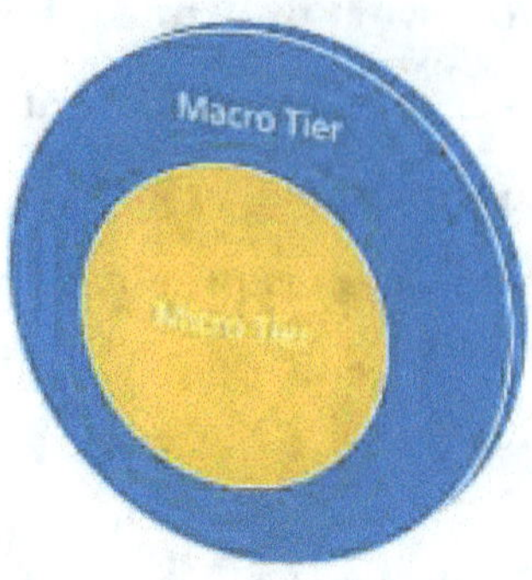

The macro tier of the ecological social system includes neighborhoods, the languages spoken, the political context, and institutional systems (schools, hospitals, religious institutions, etc). Remember that all tiers have an impact on a person's development; the micro tier has a direct impact on the person, the mezzo tier has a secondary impact through people and things in the micro tier, and the macro tier has an indirect impact on the person or family. Professional interventions on the macro level are with policy, large agencies, and funding.

The ecological social systems model is a solid foundation for professional helping and, specifically, human behavior in the social environment (Klemmer & McNamara, 2020). Neighborhoods, the languages spoken, the political context, and institutional systems (schools, hospitals, religious institutions, etc.) have an impact on the development of the individual and the family unit. Well-grounded theory helps us know what to look for in our observations, helps us to predict outcomes, and suggests helpful interventions that will bring positive change. We work toward this goal by promoting the well-being of the entire society by building healthy communities.

The role of professional helping in these interactions is to develop better adaptations for the person or group and better environments for all. Linking our services to other formal social structures, such as the legal system, education system, and health systems, combines resources to create a more efficient macro-system impact. Effectively linking our fields to other professional fields weaves a thread of interdependence into the grid of our community's foundation that promotes the health of our thriving community.

Connecting Advocacy and Collaboration for Professional Helpers

Advocates are change agents (the energy). On one end of the spectrum of definition, an attorney advocates for his client in a court of law, and on the other end, a social worker advocates for vulnerable populations that have little or no influence on their own. The attorney advocates for the best possible result for his client, and the social worker advocates for social justice and basic human needs.

Advocacy in social work entails a dual approach of case advocacy (individual level) and cause advocacy (systemic level), emphasizing the critical role of social workers in empowering marginalized communities and influencing societal policies. This aligns with the professional responsibility of advocating for those facing discrimination and social injustice (Virginia Commonwealth University, 2020). We apply our influence to improve the quality of life on behalf of a person or people who lack influence. Individuals, groups, and the greater community are all beneficiaries of his work.

Collaboration is a conduit (the pathway) for positive change. According to BMC Public Health, it can be stated that an effective mental health intervention must be consistent with societal goals and be adaptable to diverse communities and client subgroups. Interventions that demonstrate lasting results to individuals and communities require cooperation and idea-sharing between organized systems and institutions. However, it is suggested that more integrations of PMH (Public Mental Health) strategies are required for wider service providers to engage with the interventions (Fitzgerald et al., 2021).

Communities that work in silos tend to demonstrate short-term goal attainment, increased scrutiny, and higher costs associated with higher levels of care. Sharing information and ideas reduces duplication of efforts, creates accessible public services, and results in goal attainment with less intrusive interventions. Western societies currently apply case management to conduct advocacy and collaboration in the field of mental health.

Consider hospital discharges for patients with chronic illness enrolled in a Medicaid or Medicare program. Patients discharged without a plan for continued services in the community were common through the 1980s and into the 1990s. Expensive and repeated admissions soon drew the attention of administrators and politicians. Increasingly, administrators imposed structured standards related to length of stay. Patients often suffer from progressing disease, a lower quality of life, and admission to a skilled nursing facility for a longer stay. Eventually, and through advocacy efforts and collaboration between professionals in the community, it became apparent that a planned release that included outpatient appointments and in-home services improved the outcomes and saved money.

Chapter Summary

Systems of care work within the micro and the macro tiers of the ecological social system. The term direct practice often refers to clinical support for the individual and family on the micro tier. Indirect practice is the term for macro-tier interventions with the political context and institutional systems (schools, hospitals, religious institutions, etc.). Both tiers have an impact on individuals and families who survive and thrive within a community. Professional interventions on the micro level work with individuals and families directly, and our work on the macro level is with policy, agencies, and funding.

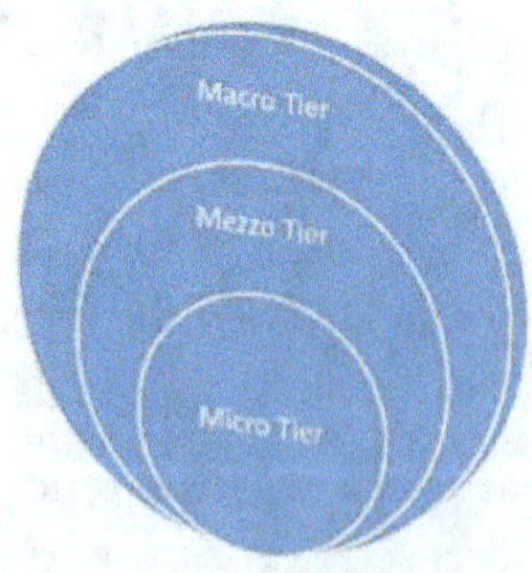

As professional helpers, we find that when we demonstrate that an intervention or policy is helpful in lessening a social problem, all parts of the ecological social system benefit. The role of a professional in these interventions is to develop better adaptations for the person or group and better environments for all. Linking social services to other formal social structures such as the legal system, the education system, health systems, and religion combines resources to create a more efficient macro-system impact. We work toward this goal by promoting the well-being of the entire society through building healthy communities.

Chapter 3

ADVOCACY IN CASE MANAGEMENT SERVICES

Introduction

Professional helping, broadly defined, is a formal process of addressing physical, emotional, psychological, or spiritual problems faced by people. Westernized cultures recognize a conventional process of training and higher education to master and sharpen research-supported skills that support professional practice. Professional advocacy through case management is the process of alleviating barriers so that people can effectively address their problems, with or without ongoing professional assistance. Often, vulnerable people groups lack the capacity to access benefits and services intended to address problems due to systemic oppression, lack of skills and resources, or contradictory policies and procedures.

Three primary outcomes support our goal of helping vulnerable people. First, we want to improve the quality of life of the vulnerable population. By helping vulnerable people groups coexist in the community, they can realize a life purpose, engage in meaningful relationships, and contribute to society. Next, reducing oppression and discrimination ensures the safety of our community. The risk of violent victimization dramatically increases based on the demographics of age, sex, ethnicity, and race. It is even more profound when compared with socioeconomic status and disability. Finally, by helping people in need, clinical interventions at a lower level of care are effective, which is less intrusive to the person and more cost-effective to society.

Professional Case Management

In advocating for individuals and families, we employ the strategy known as micro advocacy to enhance their quality of life. The essence of micro advocacy lies in fostering growth and autonomy, aiming for a future where professional support is no longer necessary. Our ultimate goal is for individuals to achieve a state of healthy interdependence within their communities—a dynamic where both the individual and the community mutually benefit and support each other.

This form of advocacy involves raising awareness about individual rights, empowering people to actively exercise these rights, and crafting opportunities for meaningful participation in decision-making processes that directly impact their lives. By focusing on these areas, we help individuals navigate and influence the social systems around them and contribute to a broader framework where advocacy is deeply embedded in everyday interactions and community engagement.

This approach to micro advocacy also evolves as we continue to navigate significant policy changes in areas like health care, housing, and family support—compounded by ongoing challenges such as the COVID-19 pandemic. This evolution is reflected in our commitment to integrating practical, real-world applications of policy that underscore the interconnectedness of individual well-being and community health (Chapin & Lewis, 2023). It also includes helping people access needed goods and services so that they can improve their quality of life and work toward self-sufficiency.

When we advocate on behalf of groups or populations, we call it macro advocacy. Here, we are cultivating change that results in social equality, social justice, and social inclusion. Social equality means that everyone has equal access to opportunities, goods, and services. An historical example is that women can register to vote just as men can. Social justice has to do with access to opportunity and goods within a society. This means that equal access requires intervention. For example, even though the law says that public schools must provide a high-quality education, they do not. This disparity is caused by many things but includes the stress of poverty of families, neighborhood safety, and the lack of parental contribution to the child and school. Advocacy for social justice insists that schools in low socioeconomic areas require extra support to make up for a lack of parental involvement and to provide incentives for good teachers. Similarly, social inclusion means that diverse members of a society feel welcome throughout the community. Examples of this include accessible and comfortable public services and institutions (religious organizations, schools, hospitals, restaurants, and work or leisure places of business).

Question 1: ___________ advocacy is when we advocate on behalf of an individual or family.

Question 2: ___________ advocacy is when we advocate on behalf of a group of people or a vulnerable population.

Professional advocacy through Case Management is deliberate and strategic, whether on the micro level or on the macro level. It requires setting a goal and planning a combination of methods and approaches to achieve that goal. In a professional setting, it means that the advocate is doing this work as part of their job and is accountable for the consequences of their work. A well-defined problem statement leads to project goals and measurable objectives. Relevant stakeholders, which include service users, policy makers, program administrators, and neighborhood residents, are included. These steps are difficult in the beginning but result in efficient work and improved outcomes for service participants.

Joining with Vulnerable People in Need

Vulnerable people groups, such as adults who suffer from serious mental illness, are at greater risk of suffering social problems and having fewer resources with which to combat or overcome these problems. This may result in separation from helpful resources, maladaptive factors (such as living in high crime rate neighborhoods) and focusing on basic needs at the expense of pursuing long-term quality of life improvement. When people can comfortably coexist in the community, they are able to realize a life purpose, engage in meaningful relationships, and contribute to society. Advocacy for vulnerable people consists of joining them in their present environment and defining the problems and barriers from their perspective. Fixing problems from our perspective is not advocacy because it removes ownership of the problem from the people suffering to someone who is not suffering.

Much of the advocacy work in case management involves alleviating barriers so that people might effectively address their problems, with or without professional assistance. When struggling to meet basic needs of shelter, safety, and rest, people may lack the capacity to access benefits and services intended to address problems. Case managers step in to link them with basic necessities, but we are also ensuring that their rights are being upheld by the people who administer the benefits. Throughout this process, advocacy combines micro support by promoting the person's involvement in the process with macro support by challenging marginalization within the community. Sharing decisions with the people we serve is critical to advocacy because the person who owns the problem must take an active role in problem mitigation. Having a professional decide how to solve a person's problem depletes that person's confidence in their ability to influence factors in their own life. The goal of advocacy in case management is for the supported person to believe and behave as if they have the capacity to influence the trajectory and outcomes in their life. Understanding our own responsibility in our situation shapes our thoughts and behavior toward choices that generally result in fewer social problems and nurturing relationships.

The involvement of clients and their caregivers in advocacy is fundamental to fostering empowerment. Empowerment emerges through a synergistic blend of active participation and the practical application of skills and knowledge. This collaborative approach not only facilitates a deeper understanding of individual rights and systemic processes but also enhances the ability of clients and their support networks to advocate effectively for their needs and aspirations. As outlined by Chapin & Lewis (2023), this method of advocacy underscores the importance of a participatory framework where clients are not passive recipients of services but active contributors to the advocacy efforts that shape their lives. Through this engagement, they gain the tools and confidence needed to navigate and influence the social policies that affect them directly. The empowerment process, therefore, is both a goal and a method achieved through continuous learning, adapting, and participating within the spheres of influence available to clients and their caregivers.

Advocacy is a partnership; both have a right and obligation to participate and reap the outcomes. The client, patient, caregiver, or other stakeholder must participate in the advocacy process.

Discussion

Why is it better to join with someone, providing support, than it is to solve their problem for them? Give three reasons.

Elements of Advocacy in Case Management

Effective social advocacy on the macro tier requires more than formal meetings, written objectives, and a carefully worded message. It requires an authentic passion for the cause. In the field of mental health, the cause is often associated with removing bureaucratic barriers and modifying policies tied to funding allocations. This requires us to form an advocacy group that mobilizes our client base, inspires stakeholders to join in, and influences policymakers to improve the identified policy or procedure. For that to happen, objective data and real-life stories must support our definition of the problem. This requires expertise, professionalism, mutual respect, and patience.

In order to change the understanding, position, and actions of people in positions of influence, we must present our demand for change with credibility and professionalism. By cultivating a sound and sustainable advocacy group, we present a foundation for carrying out and sustaining our own efforts. This is necessary to overcome a history of short-term efforts that left administrators frustrated and people in need in limbo. Growing our advocacy group, the number of participants, and the strength of our alliance provides a sound platform for increasing public awareness, adding media attention, and improving access to policy makers.

Question

Place these advocacy actions in order from micro to macro levels in the ecological social system.

Requesting that a doctor accept a specific patient with Medicaid benefits.

Encouraging a caregiver to advocate on behalf of their patient.

Meeting with an agency administrator about removing a barrier to service access.

Inviting professionals in the community to join committees to improve outcomes for a vulnerable population.

Testifying in a congressional hearing in favor of policy improvement on behalf of a vulnerable population.

Our goal is to declare human dignity and the importance of choice among people who suffer from mental illness and lack social power and influence. Our role is much broader than the stated goals of one project. One macro-level advocacy project demonstrates the power of promoting long-term good for the entire community. Throughout the project, we are modeling helpful interpersonal skills, coaching and encouraging our allies, and setting the example of compassion for all people. Demonstrating sound ethical behavior and positive moral values is critical to both our followers and to the people with influence whom we are advocating.

Professional case managers must recognize their responsibility for advocacy. This is an essential element because it proves our authenticity and the genuine value of human life. For example, our advocacy efforts may conflict with agency policy and procedure or the opinions of other professionals. An example might include an eligibility rule that creates a bureaucratic barrier to benefits or services. The point is to focus on helping people in need to shape and direct their own lives.

Sometimes, our first efforts are to improve the culture of our agency so that we can work to improve our community later. The most fruitful environment for social equality, social justice, and social inclusion is a professional culture of advocacy in both a community and its human service agencies. To cultivate this, we must facilitate stakeholder involvement from the consumer base, the neighborhood, the business community, and the community leadership. A community assessment helps us to determine the community's strengths (helpful attributes) and limitations (not helpful attributes). Part of this assessment is to answer the question, "how does the structure of policy and practice influence stakeholder input?" Stakeholder input is a measure of a healthy community.

Discussion question 2: How might you contribute to an advocacy-based agency and professional community culture?

Conclusion

Case manager advocates provide more than important advocacy support for people in need. We demonstrate to the community how we value people with problems and give cues for how everyone should likewise value them. By demonstrating how one can act to protect and defend the rights of others, we show everyone in the community that they, too, can take such action. By encouraging everyone to see that this is not "someone else's business," we demonstrate the importance of everyone in the community.

Chapter 4

ADVOCACY FOCUSED
Professional Collaboration in Case Management

Introduction

Course of action for improving outcomes for individuals and in a community must involve both advocacy and professional collaboration regarding individual cases (micro level) and regarding system-wide barriers and access to care (macro level). Professional collaboration occurs within an agency and between professionals at different agencies. Ideally, a small group of stakeholders comes together to create a plan that addresses barriers at different system levels.

Sometimes, coming together to reduce stigma and educate stakeholders is the first step. For other communities, the first step is to determine the conduits for collaboration between agencies. This process requires both a micro and a macro intervention; our efforts to improve collaboration and advocacy must address the system of care simultaneously to address the needs of individual persons.

Discussion

Think about the people you work with or that live in your neighborhood. Are some more open to helping others? Are some easier to team with? List three factors in favor of each.

What is Professional Collaboration?

Definitions of professional collaboration vary, reflecting the formality and placement within the ecological social system. At the micro level, professionals collaborate on individual cases, while at the macro level, the focus shifts to policy collaboration. The objectives of the collaboration and the relationships among the professional advocates often dictate the level of formality involved.

An expanded definition of professional collaboration, informed by recent research from Austin & Gregory (2024), underscores the importance of integrating internationally educated health professionals (IEHPs) into the healthcare workforce. The Health Human Resource Strategy department of the Canadian Government advocates for an inclusive approach that goes beyond technical competencies to encompass cultural and workplace integration. This comprehensive definition embraces widely accepted principles of professional collaboration and highlights the necessity of addressing both social/contextual skills and interprofessional practices. It stresses the importance of patient-centeredness and the adaptation of IEHPs to the professional culture within Canadian health systems, which is crucial for optimizing the delivery of patient care.

"Interprofessional collaboration in education and healthcare involves diverse health professionals working together to improve patient outcomes. It emphasizes teamwork and effective communication across disciplines, enhancing the educational and care experiences. Integrating varied perspectives and expertise ensures comprehensive patient care, effectively addressing all aspects of patient health. This inclusivity makes healthcare delivery more efficient and leverages the unique skills and experiences of each team member, including internationally educated professionals (Austin & Gregory, 2024)."

Question: Which is not collaboration?

    A. A conversation with peers about the cause of a social problem.

    B. Telling your employees what to say to professionals at another agency.

    C. Inviting the family members of clients to a "meet and greet."

    D. Attending a community meeting to define a problem related to access to healthcare.

The Purpose of Professional Collaboration

Professional collaboration exists to solve problems. It is useless without a goal and a plan. Groups may gather to solve a problem and fail to set a goal, but these groups will never gather without a task to complete. Collaborative efforts must have a purpose or a problem to solve. Advocacy-based collaboration exists to promote social justice and increase access to resources among vulnerable populations.

Professional collaboration can be formal or informal. Formal collaboration includes documentation of meetings, decisions, and procedures for carrying out the plan. Informal collaboration is primarily verbal and among professionals with great trust and respect for one another. The weight of the problem and the structure of access to influential stakeholders also affect the level of formality. Formality falls on a continuum rather than being either formal or informal. Part of the advocacy process that involves collaboration might be informal, while other parts are formal.

Question True or False? Informal collaboration is not professional.

Broadly identifying a problem or barrier as part of the collaboration is the first step. In other words, the fully defined and detailed problem is only established with input from a diverse group of stakeholders. The advocates that initiate the collaboration determine the broadly defined problem, which dictates the group of stakeholders. From there, the full group of stakeholders comes together to discuss and determine the dynamics, influences, and barriers of the problem. This definition is fluid, as is the list of stakeholders. As the collaboration advances, the scope of the problem and the collaborative group may change.

People directly impacted by the problem are stakeholders, either those who want to help or those who oppose the collaborative advocacy project. It is important to include opposing voices in thorough collaboration because a one-sided solution lacks the foundation necessary to sustain substantial change. The stakeholder group also includes those who create or implement policy and those who live or work in close proximity to either the problem or the solution. It is necessary to be inclusive without being exhaustive with the list of stakeholders. We must make sure that all perspectives are included without having meetings that lack feasibility in relation to time and participation.

Discussion: Name an agency in your community. Name five stakeholders related to the population served or the social problem.

The purpose of professional collaboration is to bring interested parties together to fully define the problem and barriers, to determine a desirable outcome, and to create measurable objectives that will help achieve the desired outcome. The findings of a study by Verhaegh, ET. Al. (2017) indicates that it is important for healthcare professionals to consider how team members and patients are involved in the decision-making process and how current social and spatial structures can affect communication and collaboration between the healthcare team and the patient (Verhaegh, Seller-Boersma, Simons, Steenbruggen, Geerlings, de Rooij, & Buurman, 2017). It is important to consider the comfort level of participants when providing input and to ensure that meetings, emails, phone calls, and other methods of collaboration are easily accessible by all parties involved in the effort.

Initiation Collaboration of an Advocacy-Focused Collaboration

The structure, formality, and coordination of advocacy-focused professional collaboration vary based on the weight, urgency, political climate, and available resources related to the problem. The situation or person that brought the problem to light influences the dynamics of the collaboration, including the motivation of the involved advocates. Sometimes, individuals within the community bring the problem to light by becoming vocal through public media or meetings. Other possibilities are that the issue is sparked by an external agency (such as a State Department) or it is raised through policy creation or modification (a new law requires collaboration to fix a problem).

When initiated by residents of a community, there is likely high motivation for a quick and sustainable solution, and discussions may be emotionally charged. If an agency initiates an advocacy-related collaboration based on the struggles of its client population, the motivation is often moderate, and the effort falls into a prioritization schedule, which may delay the achievement of project objectives. Mandated collaborations are often riddled with bureaucracy, and individual members of the collaboration have low motivation, or the project is a low priority.

Even when a service consumer or family member raises a critical issue with high motivation, the inclusion of professionals in the advocacy effort is essential. Their participation lends credibility, access to a professional network, and substantial influence, enhancing the collaborative project's effectiveness. This can be likened to a machine designed for change, where professional collaboration forms the mechanism, and the genuine commitment of the advocates serves as the fuel driving this machine forward. The role of the catalyst or initiator in these efforts is crucial; the sustainability and success of the initiative often hinge on the initiator's persistent drive and dedication. As evidenced by the systematic review of 36 studies, while the impact of such collaborations on health outcomes is mixed and generally unconvincing, the dynamics within these partnerships—such as motivation, resources, and leadership—play significant roles in shaping their functionality and potential success. This highlights the complex interplay of factors that must be managed to optimize the effectiveness of cross-sector health collaborations(Alderwick, Hutchings, Briggs, & Mays, 2021).

Goals of the Collaboration

Professional collaboration, rooted in advocacy, aims to enhance the quality of life for vulnerable populations. Effective collaborations require clearly defined, aligned goals that address both health care and non-health care needs. According to Alderwick, Hutchings, Briggs, & Mays (2021), successful partnerships often hinge on integrated services and tackling health inequalities. Understanding key factors such as motivation, purpose, and goal alignment is crucial for impacting health care and health equity effectively. For example, the effort may work toward the goal of bettering agency outcomes by improving the quality of the interventions. This might require collaborators to focus on program implementation or procedure.

Another possibility is that the collaboration is working toward the goal of improving an entire system of care. This requires the work of advocates from different agencies to focus on coordinating policy and procedure. Finally, some advocacy-focused professional collaboration seeks to change policy at the governmental level (local, state, or federal). Here, a large long-term commitment is necessary to reach citizens, professionals, administrators, and policymakers.

Professional helpers are in a key position to recognize social problems or barriers to access to problem mitigation that exist in a community. We hear our patients and clients when they express helplessness and frustration. Our first step is to track complaints and begin to identify the problem and barriers. Next, we share the collective concern with other professionals, form a group, and begin our advocacy effort. This process might take months or years.

As professionals collaborate about a community-wide problem or barrier to assistance, we begin to identify stakeholders attached to the problem. Stakeholders include the people in need of assistance, their families, people who provide assistance, and people who benefit from maintaining the problem. Collaboration involves teamwork and requires that we consider opposing and supporting points of view. Advocacy requires that we speak out in favor of the voiceless or vulnerable, who are our patients and clients. Considering the views of diverse stakeholders creates a solid foundation for sustainable change.

Political Influences

The political climate of the agency, system of care, or community plays a crucial role in how and why we engage in advocacy-based professional collaboration. From a systemic point of view, politics influences the advocacy efforts, and the advocacy influences political strategy. Politicians want to please donors and voters, who may be at odds regarding care for the poor, civic responsibility, and social justice. There is also great philosophical debate about how much government should require or provide (regulations and benefits). Politicians want to create a policy that benefits their donors and is relatively pleasing to the voting public.

Political climate is a term to describe the fluid state of comfort, opinion, and mood of a society or group of people. It may describe morale at an agency or unrest in a community. This climate is highly influenced by the culture of the society or group, which manifests itself as beliefs, attitudes, and behavior. Politics can influence a culture, but it is much more likely that the culture will influence politics. This is why advocacy is effective in influencing political decisions. When a political climate is unstable (voters could go either way), advocacy is more effective than in a climate that leans heavily toward or away from the target of the advocacy effort (Taghizadeh, 2016).

Professional helpers find themselves involved in agency, community, or governmental politics because of their code of ethics or their moral code. Advocacy in the political arena focuses on changes in policy and procedure (macro advocacy) and requires professional collaboration with people who agree with us and people who do not agree with us. Politicians are somewhere in the middle. When we need to facilitate change on the macro level, we need to carry influence and fulfill responsibilities (Warner, 2017). Our influence on others grows with our expertise and our demonstration of ethical actions that reap positive benefits for our community.

Macro-level advocacy requires a collective effort from our peers, our neighbors, and our politicians.

It requires professional collaboration. Likewise, politicians rely on professional organizations and collaborative groups to promote their message. Whether a small group within a single agency or a nationwide professional organization, we carry more power and influence in numbers. Additionally, as our patients and clients see us working in their favor, as community members watch us model community-building, and as our peers see us making progress with difficult problems, more people join in.

Question True or False? A professional helper should only advocate for individual clients and families.

Chapter Summary

Professional collaboration exists to solve problems. It may occur within an agency or between professionals in different agencies. Advocacy-based collaboration works in the interest of a vulnerable population or community. A metaphor is that professional collaboration is a machine working for change, and the authentic fight of the advocates is the fuel that powers the machine. It is important to include opposing voices as part of our collaborative advocacy because a one- sided solution lacks the foundation necessary to sustain substantial change. Politics influences our advocacy efforts, and advocacy influences political strategy. Politicians want to please donors and voters, who may be at odds regarding care for the poor, civic responsibility, and social justice.

Chapter 5

INDIVIDUAL CASE (MICRO SYSTEM): COLLABORATION IN CASE MANAGEMENT

Introduction

Micro system collaboration (individual case) is similar to macro system collaboration (discussing policy and procedure) because we are amplifying the partnership and participation of a variety of professionals who come together to explore the case. Throughout the process of micro-collaboration, we are focusing on the strengths and needs of the individual rather than the community. This allows us to agree on treatment priorities and desired outcomes for the person or family.

The primary objective of case collaboration is that the person will have access to services that are sufficient to help him or her coexist in the community in a manner that consists of safe housing, medical care, productive activity, and social nurturance. By increasing positive functioning in the eight primary life dimensions, we expect to see a decrease in criminogenic thinking and behavior.

Case Collaboration

For professional case managers, the cornerstone of case collaboration is a clear and open communication with the client. It is crucial to articulate our intentions regarding assistance and the purpose of our involvement in their situation. Conveying a clear message about our role and objectives fosters a positive rapport and provides a clear direction for the relationship. The client's perception of our effectiveness in connecting them to necessary benefits and services, our influence in professional decisions across different agencies, and our demonstrated expertise are vital components that contribute to successful interventions. This approach reflects a commitment to sophisticated, evidence-based practices that enhance the quality of interaction between social workers and clients, ensuring interventions are not only effective but also well-informed by current research methodologies (Alston, 2020).

Discussion: Have you ever been the client or patient of a professional who seemed to be more interested in having you as a client for their own purpose rather than to assist you? Have you ever worked with a professional that seemed to have your best interest in mind? Describe how you felt about both and your satisfaction with the service(s).

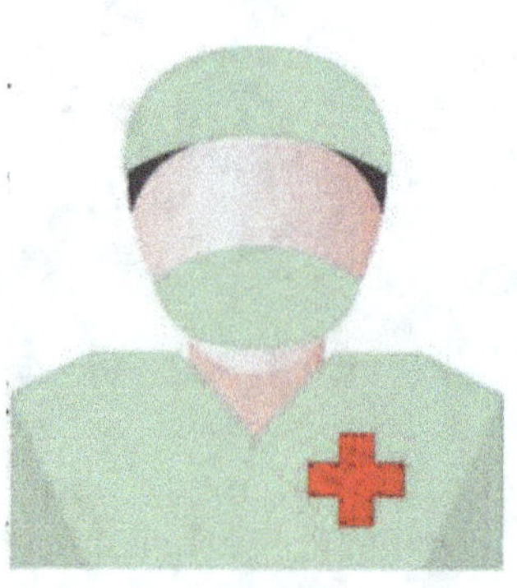

Rarely can one professional fully address the multifaceted needs of a single client. Professional roles and responsibilities are complementary, enhancing the collective capability of the team. It is essential to recognize and utilize the diverse influences, areas of expertise, and access to benefits and services that each member of our collaborative team contributes to the case. This integrated approach, as highlighted by Alston (2020), underscores the importance of leveraging varied professional perspectives to achieve comprehensive and effective client support. This requires us to build and maintain positive affiliation, keep track of key positions that change over time, and allows us to link our clients or patients with needed resources in a timely manner. The scaffolding of professional collaboration is based on a solid network in the community and creates a framework that ties direct practice in the micro tier to indirect practice in the macro tier.

As we consider the needs of an individual (or family), we tap into our existing familiarity with community resources. This requires us to track the quality, availability, and accessibility of benefits and services in our community (Turner, 2017). A wide variety of agencies, institutions, and systems of care provide these formal sources of assistance and require navigation through unique eligibility criteria, application processes, and avenues of communication. Case collaboration ties the needs of the individual with resources through a bridge between the micro and macro levels of care.

Question True or False? In most cases, one professional can meet the needs of the person or family.

Presenting Problems

A significant part of direct practice (working directly with the client) is crisis intervention because a life crisis is typically what brings a client or patient to our agency. A life crisis is essentially a significant event that causes stress and disruption in a person's life. One important characteristic of a life crisis is that it cannot be settled by applying the person's or family's usual coping strategies. Another is that the event seems threatening to the person or family and results in anxiety, fear, or other uncomfortable emotions. A life crisis highlights frailties within the family system and provides an opportunity for growth and improvement in the system (Turner, 2017).

Question: Which one is not a characteristic of a life crisis?

a. It causes disruption in a person's life.

b. It cannot be settled with the person's usual coping strategies.

c. The person or family is fearful about what might happen.

d. It is always the result of a bad choice that the person made.

Crises are common to the clientele of case managers in mental health services. Nevertheless, we want to help people reach a point where a crisis is atypical and rare rather than the norm. The focus of our intervention and referral process is on building resilience and adaptive coping skills that will prevent either the frequency of crises or the intensity of them. Because we often serve people who are enrolled in services with several agencies or systems of care, collaboration of the treatment goals and objectives is necessary to prevent incompatible action steps. It is also necessary to promote consistent expectations and prevent provider manipulation.

Case Scenario

Imagine what it might be like for a 30-year-old woman to find herself released from jail homeless and required to report to her probation officer the next day. Add the compounding factor of chronic and serious mental illness that requires medication to maintain behavioral stability and a history of removal from supportive housing services due to inappropriate and threatening behavior. Now, consider her systems of care and plans of intervention. She may see probation as her top priority in the interest of avoiding jail time, but her mental health provider believes that she will not avoid incarceration without medication to stabilize her behavior. Others view housing as her top priority.

Next, consider that the scenario becomes even more complex when her probation officer requires her to get a job, her mental health provider requires her to attend day treatment, and the judge orders her to secure housing within 30 days. Professional collaboration can improve this common scenario. Here, the client, probation officer, mental health provider, supported housing provider, and homeless shelter manager meet or exchange electronic communication about her strengths, needs, history, and situation.

A single plan of intervention sets the goal of avoiding incarceration and securing safe and stable housing. Objectives include demonstrating adaptive behavior that nurtures positive interactions with peers at the homeless shelter, following requirements and securing disability income, and abstaining from illicit drug or alcohol use. The services designed to help her meet these objectives include psychiatric treatment for medication monitoring, sheltering in the homeless shelter for 30 days, attending day treatment for adults with serious mental illness, substance abuse group therapy, and case management to coordinate care and report behavioral stability to the supported housing provider.

The coordinated plan based on professional collaboration allows the client to address her limitations with a plan that is supportive and achievable. Most importantly, if successful, the plan will result in a greatly improved quality of life for her. As the team continues to collaborate on her behavior, needs, and progress, the plan is modified to meet her needs with the hope that a housing provider will provide her with an opportunity to secure and maintain safe and stable housing.

Interventions and Supports

Direct practice with clients (micro practice) is the work we do with and for individuals and families, and indirect practice (macro practice) is the work we do with and for community agencies and systems. The focus of the collaboration delineates the type of professional collaboration that is necessary on both tiers of the social system. Micro-level collaboration focuses on helping individuals and families improve, while macro-level collaboration focuses on helping improve policy and procedure in agencies and systems of care. The two are **interdependent** upon each other; the micro system requires the macro system, and vice versa (Alston, 2020).

In addition to formal benefits and services, which require collaboration with professionals in agencies, informal benefits and services require collaboration with the client or patient's family, friends, neighbors, or other naturally occurring resources in the person's life. People who are not in our lives as professionals are the most important to us. They are also the most committed to serving our best interests long into the future. Often, people in need of professional helping find themselves estranged from friends and family due to annoying, victimizing, or dangerous behavior. Collaboration supports the reunification process and reconnects the client with the loved one. As professionals support this process, the client or patient becomes less dependent on professional services and interdependent on informal or natural supports.

Discussion: Name three people in your life that you rely on and that rely on you. What would be difficult without each person?

Strengths-Based Approach and Building Resilience

Another dynamic of micro-system collaboration that ties it to macro-system collaboration is the interaction between the individual person (and family), existing resources, and accessibility issues surrounding the connection between the two. Individuals and families have good things about them, things they are good at, supportive people around them, existing resources, jobs, housing, etc. They also have struggles, bad habits, unavoidable catastrophes, relationship problems, and financial problems. Professional helpers exist to grow the strengths and resources and minimize the problems and needs. We do this through intervention and referral and by ensuring that these benefits and services are accessible to the people who need them.

The overall purpose of human services is to help people in need improve their overall functioning in the community, at work, and at home. The concept of resilience helps us to define factors that facilitate better overall functioning in people when compared with others who experience similar circumstances. Why do some people fare well and others not so well when faced with similar circumstances?

Resilience is the ability to bounce back and overcome adversity, challenges, and tragedy.

A person with strong resilience can maintain a healthy level of functioning in the face of difficult circumstances. We might say that these people demonstrate adaptive coping behavior. At the same time, people with less resilience are more likely to experience more frequent and more intense problems and challenges in all life domains. We might say that these people demonstrate maladaptive coping behavior.

Let us delve deeper into what we mean by **adaptive coping behavior**. This behavior **leads to positive outcomes**. For professional helpers, positive outcomes mean that the person will need professional services less and less and will become more and more self-reliant. In other words, adaptive coping behavior means that they will be less likely to find themselves in challenging situations that require professional help (Turner, 2017).

When we consider maladaptive coping behavior, we are considering behavior that prevents us from achieving positive outcomes. This category of behavior reflects a desire for immediate gratification and a tendency to avoid long-term efforts toward solving problems. In other words, the maladaptive behavior results in our clients needing more and more help and services. Collectively, our overall pattern of behavior results in factors that influence our circumstances. When positive, these factors are "resilience factors". Resilience factors make it more likely that a person will bounce back rather than fall deeper into social problems. Factors are evidence of behavior patterns.

Question: Which one is not an adaptive coping behavior?

a. Taking advantage of social support.

b. Taking action.

c. Managing our emotions.

d. Mental avoidance by keeping busy with unproductive activities.

Conclusion

In summary, professional case- collaboration provides a framework for professional helpers to help clients alleviate or mitigate life stressors and offset them with protective factors that will help them bounce back when difficulties arise. People often come to us with more negative circumstances and situations than positive ones. Our job is to apply professional helping in a manner that increases the positive factors and decreases the negative factors in their life. We cannot do this alone. Through collaboration with other professionals in our own and other agencies and systems of care, we synergize our intervention regime to help our clients and patients improve their quality of life.

Chapter 6

INDIRECT (MACRO SYSTEM) INTERVENTIONS IN CASE MANAGEMENT

Professional interventions on the macro level are things that only indirectly affect an individual or family through policy, large agencies, and funding. **Remember that all tiers have an impact on a person's development; the micro tier has a direct impact on the person, and the macro tier has an indirect impact on the person or family through community services and government policy.** The mezzo tier has a secondary impact through people and things that link the micro to the macro tier. The macro tier of the ecological social system includes neighborhoods, the languages spoken, the political context, and institutional systems (school systems, healthcare systems, religious institutions, etc.).

The Evolution of Social Policy

Westernized society has seen the evolution of social policy move from neighbor helping neighbor to the complex system of financial professional Help, Product assistance, and medical care policy is the Root of housing support, education, and employment that we

41

see provided by governments today (Segal, 2016). Advocacy for vulnerable populations and the mitigation of social problems are essential components in effectively influencing the policy that dictates this system. These policies ensure the well-being of individuals and the society that exists within the macro tier of the ecological social system. In the US, the UK, Australia, and Canada, influential people who may never need or utilize such forms of support create and modify this policy (U.S. Census Bureau, 2021). Direct services and benefits provided by professionals in helping fields are linked to the legalese through macro-level advocacy and collaboration between systems of care. To be effective, we must understand the origin, history, and dynamics of the creation and implementation of social policy.

Social policy that allocates resources for benefits and services to people who suffer from mental illness originates with a societal viewpoint that a social problem exists and is significant enough to warrant public (taxpayer) assistance. When the strategic influential professionals have knowledge of and appreciate the impact on individuals and groups (families) within the population, they recognize a significant social problem.

This is an evolutionary process in which advocacy raises society's awareness and then stimulates the creation or modification of social policy. Following policy implementation, the changes impact society. Thus, society's viewpoint grows through experiencing each transformation (see Figure 3).

Societal Expectations and the Definition of "Need"

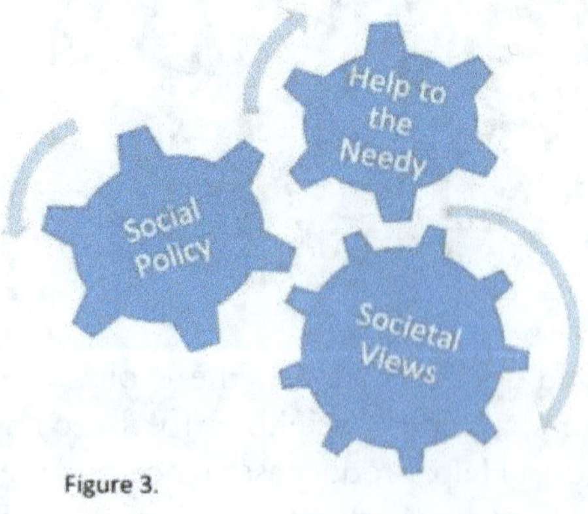

Figure 3.

For much of our history, only people with physical disabilities and those who were elderly were thought to be "worthy" of benefits or acts of charity. This means that most of the benefits people seek today would not be available to them, including benefits and services to people who suffer from mental illness. During the last century, the Great Depression, the Civil Rights Movement, and advances in psychological research have influenced societal views and social policy through advocacy. As a culture adopts new thinking, politicians produce like-minded social policies.

Prior to the Great Depression, help to the needy was guided by the principles of the Elizabethan Poor Laws, which differentiated between the "worthy" and "able." This perspective persisted through the Industrial Age, with local and state governments providing limited resources. The Great Depression significantly altered societal views on assistance eligibility, as even those previously considered "able" were unable to meet basic needs. This led to broader eligibility for aid, including those unemployed due to a lack of available jobs. As local governments struggled to cope, public support grew for federal intervention, culminating in FDR's New Deal, which redefined social welfare in the United States (Miller Center, 2020).

The Civil Rights Movement in the US had an even greater impact on our culture and public policy. The well-organized Movement gave voice to a sorely oppressed population. Activists and advocates collaborated, first with one another and eventually even the Office of the President of the United States. Eventually, tertiary groups with different approaches entered the effort. The collaborated effort and tertiary groups brought hidden injustice to light through the mass media. The result was the passage of the Civil Rights Act of 1964, which included a host of federal laws and policies that mandated social change.

Social and behavioral research influences macro-level advocacy in favor of the creation and modification of social policy. Governmental policy applies the conclusions of social and behavioral research at the local and national levels to improve how governments intervene and ensure a reasonable quality of life for their citizens. This marriage of research and policy manifests itself in two ways, first, by testing policy ideas through structured research, and second, by studying the outcomes of existing policy and programs with empirical research that applies a rigorous experimental method (Gopalan & Pirog, 2017). This research validates policy advocacy efforts and encourages collaboration by pairing like-minded systems of care that are working toward the same or a similar goal of mitigating a social problem.

An example of this historical evolution is the concept of child abuse. The term "child abuse" did not exist three generations ago. Society viewed Children as the property of their caregivers, and caregivers could treat them as they wished. Through policies designed to prevent animal cruelty, the first advocates for the care of children promoted policies that prevented child abuse (Segal, 2016). Psychological research demonstrated lasting effects on mistreated children, which enhanced the prevention and intervention policy. Today, society, in general, takes a definitive stand against cruel or excessive discipline, i.e., maltreatment of children.

Advocacy Drives Reform and Programming

Advocacy efforts are a driving force behind policy reform and the allocation of program funds. The federal government plays a significant role in providing most of the funding for state programs and sets the overarching legal framework for their use. However, state governments implement their own statutes, which allows for more granular control over policy details and procedural regulations. This layered approach to public finance is crucial in understanding the balance of power and responsibility between federal and state levels, as it directly impacts the efficacy and equity of government services and interventions (Fisher, 2022).

For example, Americans have conflicting ideas about the health care system. One motivation for reform is economic. Many believe that health care is siphoning much-needed resources from other areas of societal need, while others are of the opinion that governmental healthcare mitigates, through a ripple effect, different social concerns. Consider the tie between advocacy and the overhaul of the healthcare system. It is beneficial to have differing philosophies involved because the system is not skewed one way or the other for too long. Both sides of the political spectrum realized a need for a healthcare system overhaul. However, the debate continues about how the system should be overhauled (Campbell, 2020).

Advocacy and collaboration in the macro tier of ecological social systems play a pivotal role in the creation and modification of social policies. These policies significantly influence the operations of institutions such as schools, hospitals, churches, and government agencies. These policies not only promote economic growth and infrastructural advancements but also catalyze a paradigm shift in the perspectives of civil servants, professional helpers, and religious leaders. These macro-level social policies reshape community dynamics, enhance residents' quality of life, and underscore the necessity for sustainable and environmentally conscious development practices (Aman, Abbas, Shi, Ain, & Gu, 2022).

This, in turn, influences the neighborhood and community culture in ways that further advocacy efforts. In other words, an advocate now reaches out to concerned cohorts about a social problem. This cohort accesses its combined network to collaborate with influential others who create a conduit for the message of the advocacy effort. The message is carried throughout the community and eventually (positively influences) infiltrates policy changes and procedural mannerisms, which mitigate the identified social problem (see Figure 4).

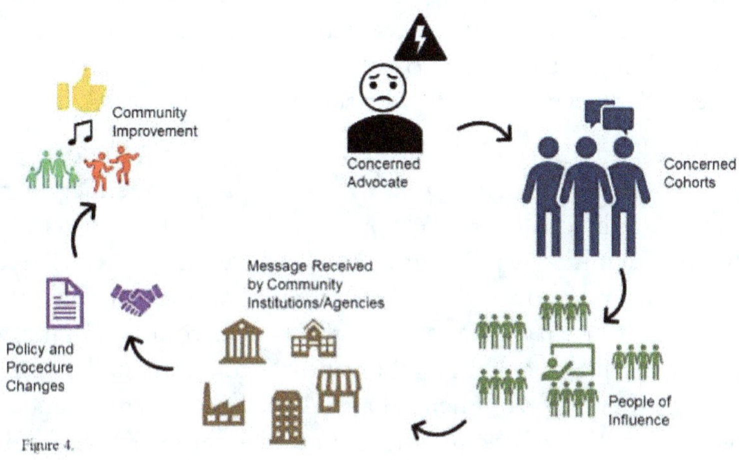

Figure 4.

The practice of professional helping at the community level includes understanding how policy addresses needs and the importance of raising awareness of the different social benefits and services to the needy, the middle class, employers, and employees. Over the years, professional helpers have used community advocacy to create and improve social policy. The National Association of Social Workers (NASW) supports involvement in policy practice that utilizes research to justify and inform policy. Advocating for policy change at the local, state, and federal levels is fundamental to advocating for the oppressed (National Association of Social Workers, 2021). Advocates ensure that needs are addressed by acting as a change agent; this is completed when we demonstrate expertise in social policy and known research that provides a conduit for policy improvement.

Case Example

As part of the routine collaboration, an independently licensed clinical social worker discussed the status of a Defendant in a competency restoration program with the Superior Court Judge. Officially restored to competence, the primary topic was the Defendant's need for mental health treatment and the risk he poses to the community if released without treatment. Further collaboration with the supervising prosecutor revealed that this was her concern, as well, and applied to multiple past and present cases. The Prosecutor then suggested, by referencing recent research, that a Mental Health Court would be a helpful part of alternative sentencing for this and other Defendants who suffer from a serious mental illness.

Recidivism is notably higher among repeat offenders with serious mental illnesses compared to non-impaired offenders. Upon release, these individuals often rely on publicly funded services and can burden communities with crime and healthcare costs. Effective reintegration support from both prison-based and community-based professionals is crucial, especially for those with complex health and identification needs, highlighting the importance of targeted assistance during and after imprisonment (Pasma, van Ginneken, Palmen, & Nieuwbeerta, 2023). Effective program and treatment coordination during incarceration and post-release is crucial for mitigating mental health issues in prisoners. This approach enhances emotional stability and reduces psychiatric symptoms both during and after imprisonment. Incorporating successful correctional-based interventions, has been shown to significantly improve mental health outcomes. Unique examples include Yoga, Seeking Safety, Transactional Analysis, Transcendental Meditation, Acceptance and Commitment Therapy, and Trauma Effect Regulation. Hidavati, et. Al. (2023) concluded that these interventions provide essential support and are instrumental in addressing the complex mental health needs of incarcerated women, ultimately aiding their rehabilitation and reintegration into society (Hidayati, Suryani, Rahayuwati, Fitrasanti, & Ahmad, 2023).

The three collaborators, a Judge, a Social Worker, and a Prosecutor, began to discuss the systemic problem in this rural community. Anecdotal observation and Court records demonstrated that people with severe mental illness co-occurring with justice system involvement are in a cycle of arrest-release-arrest. Outpatient mental health services are often inconsistent and lack coordination with the justice system and the detention facility. Based on research that demonstrates a positive correlation between outpatient mental health services and reduced recidivism, costs associated with court resources, justice advocacy, prosecution, and incarceration are preventable. With the support of the Public Defender, the Presiding Judge, and other attorneys on both sides, the group instituted a Mental Health Court to mitigate preventable crimes committed by Defendants with diagnosed mental illness.

In this county, the Mental Health Court creation and presence dramatically improved outcomes for Defendants assigned to the program. However, defendants with serious mental illness not assigned to the program continued to experience limited access and gaps in services and alternative sentencing options that result from collaboration between the two systems. It was necessary to determine a method for improving this collaboration for all Defendants with serious mental illness because not all legal teams want or find it feasible to refer to a Mental Health Court.

The Mental Health Court team considered the goal of improving outpatient service delivery and subsequently reducing recidivism to support four primary outcomes. The first is to improve the quality of life of this vulnerable population. By helping people with serious mental illness coexist in the community, they can realize a life purpose, engage in meaningful relationships, and contribute to society. Next, reducing recidivism among offenders with serious mental illness ensures the safety of our community. Many crimes committed by this population are subsequent crimes with multiple victims and result in short incarcerations followed by continuing criminal behavior. Reducing recidivism by offenders with serious mental illness will certainly lower costs associated with law enforcement, criminal defense, court proceedings, and incarceration. Finally, by addressing recidivism through service collaboration and advocacy, the clinical needs of this population were addressed with a lower level of care, which is less intrusive to the person and more cost-effective to society.

Procedure for improving outcomes in a community must involve both interagency collaboration and advocacy. As a small group of stakeholders came together to create a plan to address barriers at different system levels, advocacy associated with reducing stigma against mental illness being a mitigating factor and educating stakeholders was the first step.

The justice and mental health systems of care worked together to help all adults with serious mental illness avoid or reduce chronic justice involvement through brainstorming interventions and sentencing options that helped offenders with serious mental illness to coexist successfully in the community. Improved care resulted in less victimization, lower costs associated with incarceration and justice procedures, and severe needs addressed with an overall lower level of care. This was based on increased access to mental health services and alternative sentencing options that are only possible through collaboration.

Discussion: What are the expectations of justice professionals in terms of treatment objectives (what do they hope to accomplish)? What about service providers? What are the positive outcomes of collaboration between the justice and mental health systems that worked in favor of offenders with mental illness?

"To actually witness the collaboration at work gives us hope and confirmation that we can change the course of the mentally ill defendant's life and create a safer community for all. Those of us who have participated in the collaboration have seen the mentally ill defendant in custody. This is a person not properly medicated and often addicted to drugs and alcohol and homeless. Through collaboration, a release plan is created. The plan includes treatment, housing, and supervision based on the needs of the individual. The collaboration extends to the individual's family to ensure a system of support. The defendant becomes stabilized and is provided with the tools to become a healthy, productive member of the community, and often, we see that individual supporting others."

Lisa W. Bleich, Mental Health Court Judge, Yuma County, AZ. Retired.

With this approach, a unique opportunity where each of these groups, having a multitude of expectations, provided input and perspective that resulted in a meaningful collaboration not previously experienced. Interagency and intersystem collaboration was a positive method for helping systems develop by amplifying the partnership and participation of a range of professionals. This group of stakeholders come together to explore the macro process. In this case, they explored ways that professional collaboration improves recidivism outcomes for offenders with mental illness.

Formal help to the needy through the delivery of human services linked with the legal system weaves a thread of interdependence into the webbing of our community's foundation that ensures the health of our thriving communities. Both systems provide the societal structure by maintaining expectations of behavior and essential provisions. They frequently overlap because people in need of essential provisions often find themselves failing to meet society's expectations in terms of parenting (child protection laws and services), criminal behavior (securing resources in lawless ways), and social justice (exploitation through social power and wealth).

Conclusion

As we have seen, the essential components of advocacy in the macro tier reflect the relative changes in our societal historical patterns. The acquisition of much-needed resources otherwise not readily available is the result of advocacy from policymaking to judicial-level awareness. This has had a positive effect on individual families and other groups. The multifaceted needs of children and other vulnerable populations are met through advocacy at the macro level of the ecological social system. Through the incorporation of these various entities, we have effected positive change in the fundamental standards set for those who historically have little or no voice.

Chapter 7

COMBINING MICRO AND MACRO SYSTEM ADVOCACY AND COLLABORATION

Introduction

It is important to think about individual cases concurrently while considering the structure of community assets and resources. The assets and resources on the macro level of the ecological social tier include the healthcare system, the education system, the Courts, law enforcement, and the availability of life-sustaining resources. Often, we train professional helpers to serve the micro tier without much emphasis on the macro tier. Applying our advocacy and collaboration skills to both ensures constant quality improvement that is deliberate and purposeful and results in policy improvement that benefits the entire community.

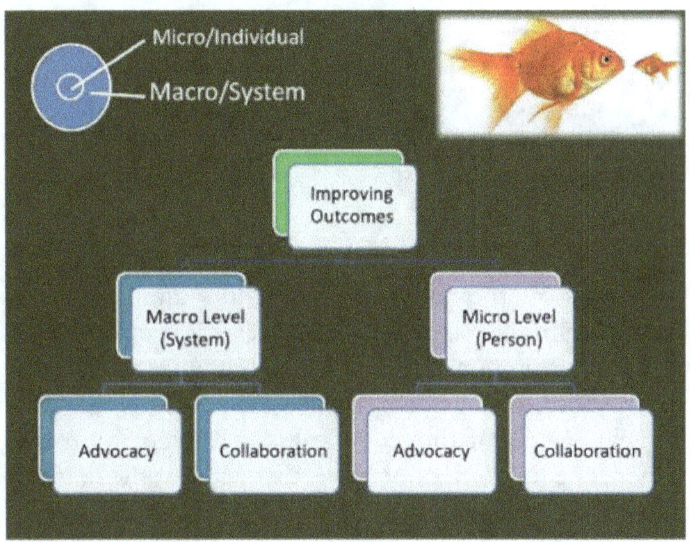

51

Building a Healthy Community

An ideal community is one with enough jobs to employ people who want them, an exchange of resources that satisfies its citizens, a lack of crime, equitable access to healthcare, education and religious practices, and disease control and prevention. The other end of the continuum would be a community with high unemployment rates, a struggling economy, high rates of crime, restrictions to healthcare, education, and religious practices, and rampant disease and illness. While all communities fall somewhere on the continuum, we generally seek to move our community toward the ideal. The Massachusetts Department of Health and Human Services (MOHHS, 2017) defines a healthy community as one in which community members join together to maintain an ongoing dialogue that fosters leadership, diversity, and a plan for the future and connects people to resources.

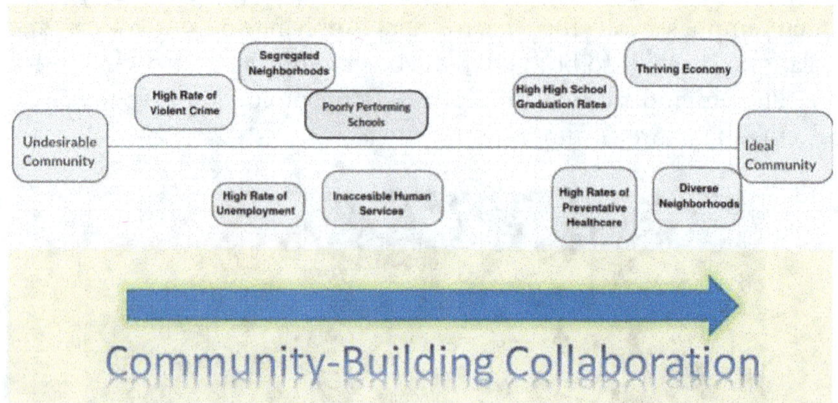

Healthy communities nurture individuals and families, and a community full of thriving individuals and families is a healthy community. Improving access to resources for individual families improves the entire community. When a community provides equitable access to resources, individual families are more likely to thrive. Intervening in one tier of the ecological social system improves factors on the other. The micro tier does not exist without the macro tier and vice versa. While some advocates focus on either the micro or the macro tier, advocacy in both tiers is necessary for a healthy community.

Consider the metaphor of water running through a faucet. Collaboration is the conduit through which advocacy runs. We cannot advocate for individual or system improvement without collaboration. The network of professionals helping individuals is a pipeline for access and continuation of care.

Continued care means that when a person goes from one place to another, they still get their prescription medication or other treatment items or services.

Through our collective work with individuals, we identify systemic problems. The micro-level network of communication becomes a grid of macro-level problem-solving. Professional helpers gain a critical perspective on the causes of social problems and are in tune with the resulting challenges for their patients or clients. We also see, up close and personal, the decrease in resiliency and lowered ability to overcome problems.

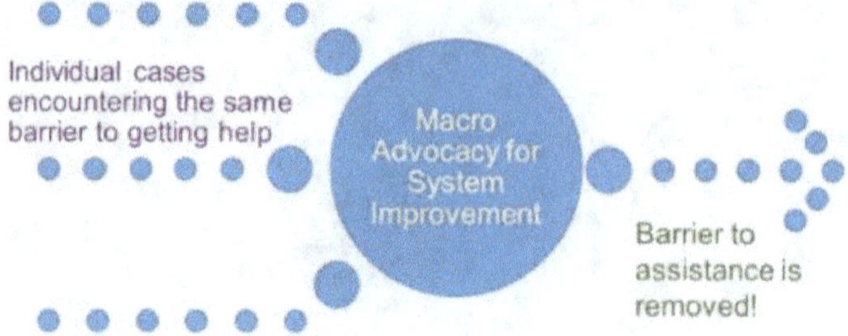

Micro-level professional helping allows us to see the ripple effect of a significant problem as well as compounding problems that develop due to system-wide failures. Structural improvements on the macro level provide a foundation for micro-level professional helping. They must go hand in hand. Our government-based formal support system (based on social policy) provides services and support to an individual or family in need. Barriers to accessing these benefits and services that repeatedly occur identify a systemic problem.

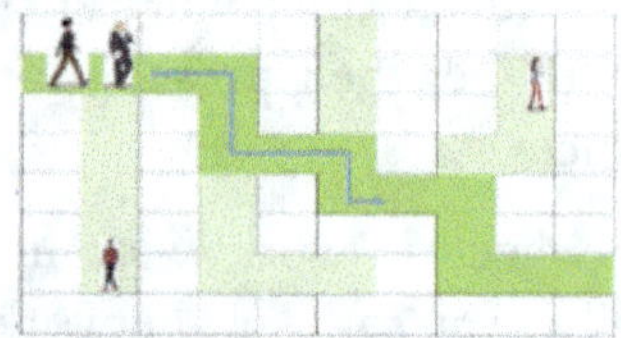

As professionals, we are aware of agency and governmental policies and procedures that define access to assistance. We understand our role in relation to the roles of our collaborative peers, as well as funding and liability issues. People in need are not aware of these complexities, so we serve as mediators between bureaucracy and the individual. Case collaboration is similar to system collaboration because we are amplifying the partnership and participation of a variety of people who come together to explore the case. Throughout the process, we are focusing on the strengths and needs of the individual. This allows us to agree on treatment priorities and desired outcomes.

The Shift from Micro to Macro Advocacy

Micro advocacy evolves into macro advocacy because we want the process to be sustained long-term. Here, we must describe the effective processes and create an ongoing procedure that may be applied to future cases. The conduit of collaboration carries all of this work through stakeholders. Stakeholders include professionals on a multidisciplinary team on the micro level and system managers and administrators on the macro level. Interagency collaboration provides a unique opportunity to brainstorm interventions from the perspectives of diverse professionals. Without such collaboration, we often see conflicting priorities and conflicting demands on the patient or client.

The primary objective of case collaboration (micro advocacy) is that the person will have access to services that are sufficient to help him or her coexist successfully in the community. Typically, by "successful," we mean in a manner that consists of minimal suffering, safe housing, medical care, productive activity, and social nurturance. For individuals, it is important to engage in specific behavior that culminates in a healthy lifestyle that builds resilience in each life dimension in order to gain and maintain these things.

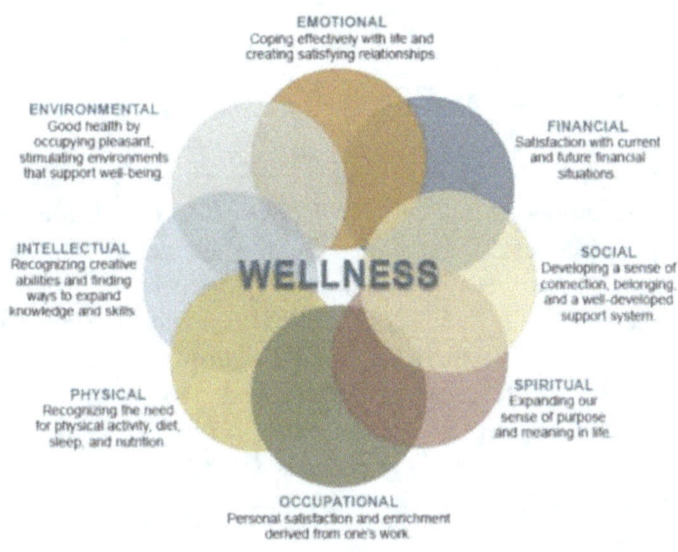

By enhancing adaptive behavior across the eight primary life dimensions anticipate a reduction in maladaptive behavior. Adaptive behavior effectively addresses and resolves immediate issues, thereby preventing larger future complications. Conversely, maladaptive behavior exacerbates existing problems without offering effective solutions for the immediate challenges. This understanding informs our approach to behavior management, emphasizing the cultivation of adaptive skills to foster long-term stability and wellness (Vaessen et al., 2023). Examples of adaptive behavior include getting along with others, showing up to work or school every day and on time, eating a healthy diet, keeping a clean home, and budgeting one's resources strategically. Maladaptive behaviors are things like not fulfilling responsibilities such as going to work or school, abusing alcohol or drugs, exhibiting anger outbursts, breaking the law, and not paying your bills.

Micro advocacy helps individuals and families to increase adaptive behavior by educating the person about the results of choices and by linking the person to resources that nurture a healthy lifestyle. Macro advocacy goes a step further by educating the entire community (outreach) and by ensuring reasonable access to resources that nurture healthy choices. Often, professional helpers on the micro level (serving individuals and families) see gaps in access to healthy choices that lead to adaptive behavior and then come together to advocate (macro level) for community improvement.

Community Building Efforts

Community building requires the efforts of many, and we cannot do it alone! Along with a collective effort comes the benefit of diverse perspectives. This includes the perspectives of people in need of benefits and services in addition to residents in the neighborhood where the effort is taking place. It also includes the efforts of professional helpers such as medical professionals, counselors, attorneys, law enforcement, and social workers. Diversity of professional roles in the community provides ready access to information about strengths and needs as well as expertise related to workable solutions.

"Outreach is defined as reaching out to others or becoming involved in a community or effort. When an organization reaches out to citizens in a community to help them find food and shelter, this is an example of outreach."

http://www.yourdictionary.com/outreach#yoAEmKCUOm DMawiv.99

Community building is a collaborative effort with a diversity of outreach conduits. Remember that collaboration is the conduit of advocacy. It is the vehicle that carries advocacy from people in need to people who can help fix the problem. Collaboration involves hearing both sides of a debate, determining common goals and objectives, considering both sides' points, and then determining a procedure that is feasible for all stakeholders and agencies. Our efforts to improve collaboration and advocacy must address the system of care simultaneously to address the needs of individual persons.

On the micro or direct service level, collaboration and the clinical interventions that result must be: clearly defined, reflect the client's goals, comply with social objectives, and demonstrate effectiveness.

We also want our interventions to have a negligible negative impact, reap positive long-term results, have a relatively low cost, be comparatively easy to implement, and be adapted to a diverse subgroup of clients and communities.

Objectives of macro or system-level collaboration include: defining effective practice associated with collaboration between systems, identify risk factors that community building can be mitigated, and defining the roles and responsibilities of the professionals who will collaborate to make it happen.

Meeting these objectives requires a diversity of influence on levels of the ecological social system. For example, the people in need of assistance do not carry great influence, yet they are paired, as part of this process, with judges, administrators, high-ranking law enforcement, and policymakers in order to develop a long-lasting and effective plan for improvement.

Bringing Micro Advocacy to the Macro Tier

Collective individual needs are "needs" that
many people share. In other words, many
people need the same thing.

This process commonly occurs but is rarely identified. Through our day-to-day work, we identify a need in our community or a barrier to accessing services and benefits. Excessive bureaucracy, in which a vulnerable person who feels helpless and hopeless does not have the wherewithal to navigate, often overshadows the need for access to legal, medical, psychiatric, vocational, and substance abuse treatment. As part of our job, we talk to each other and discover comparable conclusions about systemic or collective individuals.

Next, we formalize a plan to work toward change and invite others to join our efforts. Collaboration between the two systems involves defining what the process of collaboration will look like for this community. It will differ based on the community, the agencies, and the professionals involved. Each situation is a little different, but the overall structure of collaboration is the same.

Six Steps	Micro Level	Macro Level	Other
1. Define Barriers and Needs.	Bureaucracy, Turf Issues, Funder Expectations, etc.	Lost Support, Secure Basic Needs, SA, etc.	Staff turnover, Current Events, etc.
2. Assess Resources to Address Barriers and Needs.	Strong Leaders, Combined Funds, Community Support, Outreach conduits.	Natural Supports, Public Benefits, Service Hx, etc.	Advocates in other communities
3. Brainstorm, Outreach, Education.	Review Case Examples, Examine solution options.	Communication is key! Involve natural supports.	Stakeholder Meetings.
4. Determine a Collaborative Plan	Consensus, Funding, Assign Responsibilities	Combine Treatment Plans	Accountability Plan
5. Follow the Plan Through.	Track unintended consequences, problem-solve unexpected issues.	Support the person, Encourage, Be Reliable	Expect the unexpected!
6. Evaluate the Outcomes/Tweak Plan.	Ongoing quarterly meetings.	Regular Team Meetings, Transition out of Services	Hold each other Accountable

Here, the author is proposing a more formal process in the interest of promoting sustainable change that is feasible in any community. First, we need to define the barriers that are the purpose of our advocacy efforts. This may include agency turf issues, failure to share necessary information in a timely manner, and gaps in service delivery due to program drift. Sometimes, the agency's funders inadvertently feed this problem with complicated eligibility criteria or unrealistic program goals.

Program drift

The gradual deviation of a program from its

original design, as the program is implemented

(SAMHSA, 2017).

In Step Two, we must look at ways to overcome the barriers; we look at each tier of the ecological system. On the macro level, we find a few strong leaders creative ways to combine funds and existing community support. As we explore outreach conduits, we often find family members who want to become involved but previously did not know how, as well as professionals who thought others were addressing the problem or that they were not able to have an impact. On the micro level, we look to previous natural supports that are simply tired of the problems.

Natural supports are people who help their relatives

or friends and are not paid to do so. We all need

natural supports in order to exist interdependently

in society. We rely on others and others rely on us.

Often, with our support, these families reunify and are willing to team with the person and the professionals involved. We are also able to help the person navigate the system of public benefits and other available supportive services. Finally, don't forget about advocates in other communities. Even if they are 2000 miles away, we can share ideas, media, and success stories.

Step Three is where, as a group, interested stakeholders advocate for a vulnerable population through brainstorming, outreach to professionals and community services, and educating the public. The suggestions that result will improve the social problem or barrier to services by proposing recommendations for improving practices and policy. Ultimately, we hope that this will stimulate a collaborative partnership of stakeholders wishing to work together on an ongoing basis to improve the community's social infrastructure.

As the advocacy group becomes more active, we need to develop a plan. In Step Four, consensus cultivates a commitment to the plan. This is critical for effective and efficient community building. Without it, maladaptations such as meetings about meetings develop, and corruption might seep through cracks in the accord. Also, funding sources often look for commitment and formal collaboration. It may be necessary to secure funds in order to proceed. Next, we assign group members to specific action steps that will help move the plan forward.

As we follow through on carrying out the plan of formal advocacy through collaboration, Step Five involves monitoring the implementation and coming together to resolve unexpected challenges or unintended consequences. The population we advocate for is often involved with several agencies; we may need to push for a combined treatment plan for these individuals. Identifying a sub-group to brainstorm and work through this type of challenge is one solution.

Finally, in Step Six, we hold the service providers accountable for the delivery of the services and other stakeholders accountable for their commitments. On a primarily macro level, we need to track our progress in terms of system improvement. The ongoing process of meeting one objective results in identifying a new one. On a micro/case level, we must remember to support the person and his or her life goals. As we encourage success and prove to be reliable assistance, the person begins to believe that 'better' is possible. No case is the same! You will always hear a life story that you have never heard before and will have case scenarios that you never dreamed of; evaluate the outcomes and tweak the plan.

Conclusion

In this chapter, we walked through the application of combining advocacy and collaboration at micro and macro levels. By combining advocacy and collaboration on an individual case and then on a system-wide scale, the quality of life for people in need is improved, and the community functions in a safe and productive manner.

Chapter 8

APPLICATION: INTEGRATING MEDICAL CARE WITH MENTAL HEALTH TREATMENT

Introduction

Experts have long advocated for integrating medical and mental health care to address medication safety challenges in primary care for patients with mental illness. Recent reviews emphasize the need for targeted interventions and stronger collaboration between general practitioners and mental health specialists to improve medication adherence and safety, highlighting areas for further research and intervention development (Ayre, Lewis, & Keers, 2023). Research across both psychosocial and biological fields has consistently concluded that mental illness exacerbates physical health problems, and physical conditions can likewise worsen mental health outcomes. This interplay emphasizes the importance of adopting a biopsychosocial model to fully understand and address the complexities of health issues across genders.

Considering findings that gender differences in anxiety are influenced by a combination of brain structures, genetic factors, hormonal fluctuations, and social roles, it is clear that both biological and psychosocial factors are pivotal in shaping these health outcomes. This comprehensive approach acknowledges the intricate relationship

62

between mental and physical health, reinforcing the need for holistic health strategies that consider both biological and psychosocial dimensions (Farhane-Medina, Luque, Tabernero, & Castillo-Mayén, 2022). While physicians traditionally focus on physical diseases and dysfunctions, mental health clinicians have typically operated within a distinct care framework. However, best practice models now increasingly advocate for an integrated approach to health care, emphasizing collaboration between physical and mental health systems. Despite this recommendation, the implementation of such integrated care has been hindered by political and economic obstacles. Recent studies underscore that while progress has been slow, there is growing recognition and efforts towards establishing more cohesive and comprehensive healthcare systems that bridge the gap between physical and mental health disciplines (Bemme & Kirmayer, 2020).

The Center for Medicaid Systems (CMS) and the Substance Abuse and Mental Health Services Administration (SAMHSA) oversee federal policy and appropriations. This translates into direct services for the most vulnerable populations in the US. This chapter examines what this means for healthcare providers and patients and then describes primary methods of integrating care through applied advocacy and collaboration.

Integrated healthcare is an ideal application of the importance of combining collaboration and advocacy in professional helping because of the dramatic improvement in health outcomes and quality of life for patients who have benefited from this model. Professional helpers in the medical, mental health, and human service fields have long scrutinized the negative outcomes of treating health problems without regard to emotional well-being and of treating mental illness without regard to co-occurring physical illness. Anecdotally, we have noticed the suffering and high costs of serving people who cycle from hospital care to psychiatric care and, often, incarceration. **Changes in**

paradigm, eligibility for covered care, and policy requiring coordination have dramatically improved outcomes and are the result of micro and macro-level advocacy combined with community-wide collaboration.

Discussion: What might be a reason for increased problems after being released from jail or prison? What about from a hospital?

Struggling Healthcare System in the US

In a 2021 National Healthcare Quality and Disparities Report, it was stated that the U.S. healthcare system exists with several disparities in terms of accessibility and quality. It particularly affects racial and ethnic minorities, low-income groups, and rural populations. In a recent report by the International Health Care System Profiles by the Commonwealth Fund it was revealed that the U.S. healthcare system faces significant challenges in terms of access, efficiency, and equity compared to other high-income countries. The U.S. spends more on healthcare per capita than any other nation, yet it consistently ranks poorly on measures of healthcare access and quality. The healthcare system in the US evolved from a simple form of private health insurance in the late 1800s into a highly complicated system with fragmented payors and eligibility criteria. Much of the complications stem from detached systems that treat one aspect of a person's health. Payors that prefer volume to quality care reward providers for failing to coordinate and communicate with other healthcare systems (Stanhope & Straussner, 2017). This contrasts with what we know about the influence of environment and behavior on overall health.

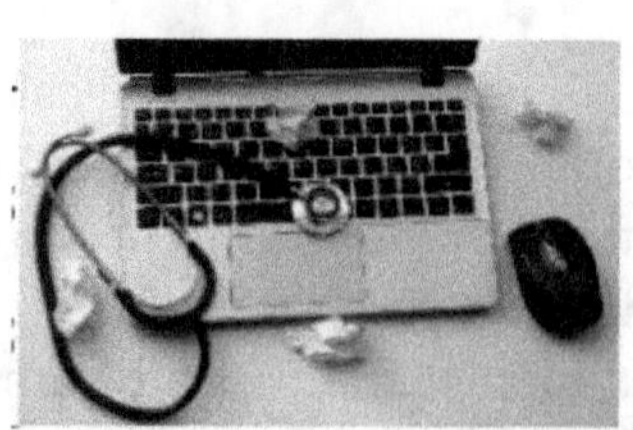

The ecological social system theory defines this phenomenon as the homeostasis that results from the influence of the environment on individuals. People with co-occurring mental and physical health problems (many also suffer from substance misuse) find themselves using hospital emergency care or psychiatric crisis services because lower levels of care are inadequate to meet their compounding needs. Chronic and significant problems create a vulnerability in which lower resilience exacerbates the likelihood of needing a higher level of care. **Frequent need for institutional care in hospitals or jails precede challenging transitions from an institution to the community**. These transitions result in more compounding problems when each system prescribes a different plan of care that often disregards feasibility issues associated with carrying out the plan. The result is a cycle of institutionalization, release, and re-institutionalization.

Discussion: How might improving advocacy and collaboration among outpatient medical and mental health services prevent hospitalization?

"Social determinants of health" refer to nonmedical. Factors that impact health include health-related knowledge, beliefs, attitudes, behavior, living and working conditions, and economic and social resources (Stanhope & Straussner, 2017). Siloed systems of care create barriers to preventative and acute treatment, which exacerbates a challenging system of health insurance coverage. First, many Americans find it difficult to secure health insurance coverage. Next, the coverage plans often restrict the types of services offered and are not accepted by all healthcare providers.

Evolution of Integrated Health and Mental Health Care

Around 25% of the adult population suffers from a mental health condition, and 68% of them suffer from a comorbid medical condition. Readmission rates in psychiatric patients are high, and physical comorbidity could be one important risk factor for psychiatric readmission (Šprah, Dernovsek, Wahlbeck, & Haaramo, 2017). This population demonstrates a disproportionate need for medical and psychiatric care, which comprises around 44% of the entire Medicaid budget in the US (Stanhope & Straussner, 2017). **Risk factors such as tobacco use, substance misuse, a sedentary lifestyle, and unhealthy eating habits aggravate the comorbidity.**

The most common and significant of these risk factors is substance misuse, and the relationship between mental illness and substance misuse matches the metaphor of "Which came first, the chicken or the egg?" One might argue that people who suffer from mental illness are likely to self-medicate through the misuse of substances, and the misuse of substances causes mental illness. Either way, **people with co-occurring medical and mental disorders experience higher rates of unemployment, homelessness, incarceration, and the lack of social support than those who suffer from one category of illness** (Stanhope & Straussner, 2017).

In recent years, we have recognized the phenomenon of co-occurring mental and medical illness, but the system of care that treats each disease separately has evolved since the late 1800s. Today, most states and local governments have separate departments for behavioral health and physical health, and substance misuse is only recently part of the public health discussion. Categorizing care in separate systems includes the same categories of funding eligibility.

The failure to tie co-occurring illness to the patient and treat the whole person results in high rates of re-hospitalization and very high costs, and the process is reinforced by a fee-for-service payment policy that incentivizes service frequency rather than service quality (Stanhope & Straussner, 2017). Healthcare policy improvement has focused on creating a system that aims at treating the whole person and focuses on preventing high levels of care. This process also intends to consider the traditional health insurance provided for the labor force alongside entitlement-related healthcare for vulnerable populations who cannot access traditional health insurance.

Discussion While both sides of the political spectrum agree that we need major policy improvement in the US healthcare system, there is great debate about how that improvement should look. Why do you think this is such a great debate?

Evidenced-Based Practice for Integrating Mental and Physical Healthcare

The idea of coordinating physical and mental healthcare along with treatment for substance misuse has proven effective in improving the quality of life of patients and in lowering the costs to society by treating illness at a lower level of care. When authenticated, this method recognizes a fundamental connection between our mind and our body. **This method also promotes quality care that includes the person's family and other natural support systems.** Empowering the person and their family prepares them to manage their own health and healthcare (Stanhope & Straussner, 2017).

The integrated healthcare model fulfills the need for mental health, substance misuse, and physical health problems as part of a whole person, and it prevents fragmented care. The US healthcare system has formalized the model, and it considers the relationship between the patient, healthcare providers, and the patient's family to be a united approach to healing compounded problems. The process also acknowledges the benefits of physical health providers and behavioral health clinicians working together with patients and their families. This process manifests itself as one-stop healthcare offices, care teams for all patients, or a case management or care coordination model that oversees all aspects of the person's care. **The use of professionals from multiple specialties addresses the needs of a whole person and improves outcomes in all areas** (Stanhope & Straussner, 2017).

The Substance Abuse and Mental Health Services Administration (SAMHSA) has endorsed the Screening, Brief Intervention, and Referral to Treatment (SBIRT) protocol for all professional healthcare services. This SAMHSA-recommended protocol is based on Motivational Interviewing (MI) and may be incorporated at all levels of care, including by paraprofessionals (SAMHSA, 2011). It standardizes the screening and referral process from the person's primary care physician, taking into account their emotional well-being.

Person-Centered Approach

In recent years, the Institute of Medicine (IOM) promoted the idea of **person-centered care, which focuses on incorporating the patient's own values, preferences, and beliefs into the plan of care**. This approach applies to physical healthcare, mental healthcare, and substance misuse treatment and prevention and incorporates a multi-disciplinary team into the assessment and treatment planning process. **The team approach prevents fragmented care and recognizes the interdependence of each specialty** in the care plan (Stanhope & Straussner, 2017). The multi-disciplinary approach also provides diverse perspectives, including the perspective of the person and natural supports, which results in a thorough treatment regimen with buy-in and shared decision-making.

Improving broad healthcare outcomes requires advocacy and collaboration from an interdisciplinary team that includes the person and their natural support system. Genuine commitment from all team members fortifies this process, and the method of person-centered care integrates the expertise of multiple specialties. Mutual respect is inherent in this process, and openly sharing ideas creates an environment of education and quality improvement. The process also produces accountability for each team member for the outcomes.

Chapter Summary

Integrated healthcare demonstrates the importance of combining collaboration and advocacy in professional helping. This model has proven a dramatic improvement in physical and mental health outcomes and in quality of life for patients. Professional helpers in the medical, mental health, and human service fields have noticed the suffering and high costs of serving people who cycle from hospital care to psychiatric care and, often, incarceration. Changes in paradigm, eligibility for covered care, and policy requiring coordination have dramatically improved outcomes and are the result of micro and macro-level advocacy combined with community-wide collaboration.

References

Alderwick, H., Hutchings, A., Briggs, A., & Mays, N. (2021). The impacts of collaboration between local health care and non-health care organizations and factors shaping how they work: a systematic review of reviews. BMC Public Health, 21, 1-16.

Hickel, J. (2020). The sustainable development index: Measuring the ecological efficiency of human development in the anthropocene. *Ecological economics*, *167*, 106331.

Gruber, J., Prinstein, M. J., Clark, L. A., Rottenberg, J., Abramowitz, J. S., Albano, A. M., ... & Weinstock, L. M. (2021). Mental health and clinical psychological science in the time of COVID-19: Challenges, opportunities, and a call to action. *American Psychologist*, *76*(3), 409.

Dhir, S., & Dhir, S. (2020). A strategic management process: The role of decision-making style and organisational performance. Emerald Insight.

Bemme, D., & Kirmayer, L. J. (2020). Global mental health: interdisciplinary challenges for a field in motion. *Transcultural Psychiatry*, *57*(1), 3-18.

Corby, Brian (2006). Applying Research to Social Work. Retrieved from http://site.ebrary.com.library.capella.edu/lib/capella/ docDetail.action?docID=10197037

Klemmer, C. L., & McNamara, K. A. (2020). Deep ecology and ecofeminism: Social work to address global environmental crisis. *Affilia*, *35*(4), 503-515.

Chapin, R. K., & Lewis, M. (2023). Social policy for effective practice: A strengths approach. Routledge.

Davis, K., Stremikis, K., Squires, D., & Schoen, C. (2014). Mirror, mirror, on the wall: How the performance of the US healthcare system compares internationally. The Commonwealth Fund. Pub. No. 1755. New York, NY.

Hittinger, R. (2020). *Critique of the New Natural Law Theory*. University of Notre Dame Press.

Evidence Supporting the Effort of an SBIRT. (2011). Screening, brief intervention, and referral to treatment. Substance Abuse and Mental Health Service Administration (SAMHSA). White Paper, Retrieved from:
https://www.samhsa.gov/sites/default/files/sbirtwhitepaper_O.pdf

Ayre, M. J., Lewis, P. J., & Keers, R. N. (2023). Understanding the medication safety challenges for patients with mental illness in primary care: a scoping review. *BMC psychiatry*, *23*(1), 417.

Fisher, R. C. (2022). State and local public finance. Routledge.

Gibbs, A. (2001). The Changing Nature and Context of Social Work Research. British Journal of Social Work, 31(5), 687. Retrieved from EBSCOhost.

Pasma, A. J., van Ginneken, E. F., Palmen, H., & Nieuwbeerta, P. (2023). Do prisoners with reintegration needs receive relevant professional assistance?. *International Journal of Offender Therapy and Comparative Criminology*, *67*(2-3), 247-269.

Gopalan, M., & Pirog, M. (2017). Applying behavioral insights in policy analysis: Trends in the United States. The Policy Studies Journal, Vol. 45, No S1.

Fishback, P. V. (2020). Social Insurance and Public Assistance in the Twentieth-Century United States: 2019 Presidential Address for the Economic History Association (No. w26938). National Bureau of Economic Research.

Austin, Z., & Gregory, P. A. (2024). Enhancing Integration of Internationally Educated Health Professionals in the Healthcare Workforce: Implications for Regulators. *Journal of Nursing Regulation*, *15*(1), 24-32.

Campbell, C. (2020). Social capital, social movements and global public health: Fighting for health-enabling contexts in marginalised settings. *Social Science & Medicine*, *257*, 112153.

Howe, D. (2009). A brief introduction to social work theory. New York, NY: Palgrave Macmillan.

Hower, J. E. (2016). "The Sparrows and the Horses": Daniel Patrick Moynihan, the Family Assistance Plan, and the Liberal Critique of Government Workers, 1955-1977. Journal Of Policy History, 28(2), 256-289. doi:10.1017/S0898030616000063

Hutchison, E.D. (2005) "The Life Course Perspective: A Promising Approach for Bridging the Micro and Macro Worlds for Social Workers". Families in Society, volume 86, issue 1, pages 143- 152.

Jordon, J., & Cooper, P.M. (2016). Building bridges: How to share research about children and youth with policymakers. Child Trends Research Brief. Pub. 2016-56.

King, S. A., & Jones, P. (2016). Testifying for the Poor: Epistolary Advocates and the Negotiation of Parochial Relief in England, 1800-1834. Journal Of Social History, 49(4), 784-807. doi:10.1093/jsh/shv092

Koontz, T, & Moore Johnson, E. (2004). One size does not fit all: Matching breadth of stakeholder participation to watershed group accomplishments. Kluwer Academic Publishers. Policy Sciences, 37:185-204.

Kuklinski, M. R., Oesterle, S., Briney, J. S., & Hawkins, J. D. (2021). Long-term impacts and benefit–cost analysis of the communities that care prevention system at age 23, 12 years after baseline. *Prevention Science, 22*(4), 452-463.

Nash, M., O'Donoghue, K., Munford, R. (2005). Chapter 1 "The Ecological Systems Metaphor in Australasia". Social Work Theories in Action (pp.32-49). London and Philadelphia: Jessica Kingsley Publishers.

National Association of Social Workers. (2021). 2021 revised NASW Code of Ethics is now in effect. Retrieved from https://www.naswnc.org/news/568202/2021-Revised-NASW-Code-of-Ethics-is-now-in-effect.htm

National Healthy Community Principles. (2017). Massachusetts Office of Health and Human Services (MOHHS). Community Health Network Areas. Retrieved from: http://www.mass.gov/eohhs/gov/departments/dph/programs/admin/comm-office/chna/healthy-community-principles.html

Opal, J. M. (2008). The Labors of Liberality: Christian Benevolence and National Prejudice in the American Founding. Journal Of American History, 94(4), 1082-1107.

Fook, J. (2022). Social work: A critical approach to practice.

Roberson, R. (2016). Enlightened Piety during the Age of Benevolence: The Christian Knowledge Movement in the British Atlantic World. Church History, 85(2), 246-274, doi:10.1017/S0009640716000391

Farhane-Medina, N. Z., Luque, B., Tabernero, C., & Castillo-Mayén, R. (2022). Factors associated with gender and sex differences in anxiety prevalence and comorbidity: A systematic review. Science Progress, 105(4), 00368504221135469.

Substance Abuse and Mental Health Services Administration (SAMHSA). (2017). Glossary of terms. Learning Center Resources Library. Retrieved from: https://nrepp-learning.samhsa.gov/glossary#P

Segal, E. A. (2016). Social welfare policy and social programs: A values perspective. (4th ed.). Boston: Cengage Learning

Vaessen, T., Reininghaus, U., van Aubel, E., Beijer-Klippel, A., Steinhart, H., Myin-Germeys, I., & Waltz, J. (2023). Neural correlates of daily-life affective stress reactivity in early psychosis: A study combining functional MRI and experience sampling methodology. *Schizophrenia Research, 255*, 93-101.

Shier, M., & Handy, F. (2015). From Advocacy to Social Innovation: A Typology of Social Change Efforts by Nonprofits. Voluntas:

International Journal Of Voluntary & Nonprofit Organizations, 26(6), 2581-2603. doi:10.1007/911266-014-9535-1

Smith, T. (2017). Homeostasis in the family or organization. www.drtomcares.com/homeostasis.html.

Sprah, I., Dernovsek, M. Z., Wahlbeck, K., & Haaramo, P. (2017). Psychiatric readmissions and their association with physical comorbidity: a systematic literature review. BMC Psychiatry, 171-17. doi:10.1186/12888-016-1172-3

Stahl, R., & Shdaimah, C. (2008). Collaboration between community advocates and academic researchers: Scientific advocacy or political research. British Journal of Social Work, 38(8), 1610-1629.

Stanhope, V. & Straussner, S. (2017). Social work and integrated health care: from policy to practice and back. New York: Oxford University Press.

Sugimoto-Matsuda, J. J., & Braun, K. L. (2014). The role of collaboration in facilitating policy change in youth violence prevention: a review of the literature. Prevention Science: The Official Journal Of The Society For Prevention Research, 15(2), 194-204. doi:10.1007/s11121-013-0369-7

Alston, M. (2020). Research for social workers: An introduction to methods. Routledge.

Taghizadeh, J. L. (2016). Are Political Parties More Responsive to Advocacy Groups Mobilising Core Voters or Swing Voters? Political Responsiveness to Citizens' Protest Movements in Swedish Local Governments. Scandinavian Political Studies, 39(2), 161-184. doi:10.1111/1467-9477.12061

Hidayati, N. O., Suryani, S., Rahayuwati, L., Fitrasanti, B. I., & Ahmad, C. A. (2023). A Scoping Review of Correctional-Based Interventions for Women Prisoners with Mental Health Problems. *Social Sciences*, *12*(8), 452.

Sutcliffe, A. (2023). HUME, HISTORY, AND THE USES OF SYMPATHY. *History and Theory*, *62*(1), 62-87.

Turner, F. (2017). Social work treatment: Interlocking theoretical approaches. 6th Edition. Oxford Press. New York, NY. ISBN: 978-0-19-023959-6.

Urie Bronfenbrenner's Ecological Systems Theory of Child Development. (2016). Health Research Funding.org (HRF). Retrieved from: http://healthresearchfunding.org/urie-bronfenbrenners-ecological-systems-theory-of-child-development/

Aman, J., Abbas, J., Shi, G., Ain, N. U., & Gu, L. (2022). Community wellbeing under China-Pakistan economic corridor: role of social, economic, cultural, and educational factors in improving residents' quality of life. *Frontiers in Psychology*, *12*, 816592.

Verhaegh, K., Seller-Boersma, A., Simons, R., Steenbruggen, S., Geerlings, S., de Rooij, S., & Buurman, B. (2017). An exploratory study of healthcare professionals' perceptions of interprofessional communication and collaboration. Journal of Interprofessional Care, 31:3, 397-400, DOI: 10.1080/13561820.2017.1289158

Warner, S. (2017). Getting political about patient advocacy. Nursing 2017. Volume 47:11. DOI-10.1097/01.NURSE.0000525989.51732.b6

U.S. Census Bureau. (2021). *Health Insurance Coverage in the United States: 2020.* Retrieved from https://www.census.gov/library/publications/2021/demo/p60-274.html

Shah-Kazemi, R. (2022). *Loving compassion in Islam and Buddhism: Rahma and Karuna.* The Institute of Ismaili Studies. Retrieved from https://www.iis.ac.uk/learning-centre/scholarly-contributions/academic-articles/loving-compassion-in-islam-and-buddhism-rahma-and-karuna/

Fitzgerald, N., Uny, I., Brown, A., Eadie, D., Ford, A., Lewsey, J., & Stead, M. (2021). Managing COVID-19 transmission risks in bars: an interview and observation study. *BMC Public Health*, 21, 11741. https://bmcpublichealth.biomedcentral.com/articles/10.1186/s12889-021-11741-5

National Archives and Records Administration. (1931). Unemployed men queued outside a depression soup kitchen opened in Chicago by Al Capone [Photograph].

www.ingramcontent.com/pod-product-compliance
Lightning Source LLC
Chambersburg PA
CBHW061301250726
48653CB00002B/720

9798338539644